Praise for *Mastering the Complex Sale, Second Edition*

 s book is a 'must-read' for anyone in the world of complex sales. Expect game
 nging impact. My team was able to improve close ratios by 20 percent by apply-
 principles in this book. Collaboration and co-creation drive much better results."

 rank Bernieri, Division Vice President, ADP, Inc.

 he clear and powerful message of this book is: Sales is a vehicle for organizational
 ange. Companies evolving to face complexity need a new kind of sales to serve
 ew kinds of customers. Jeff Thull explains why and how, with a foot in the tradi-
 ional sales world, a foot in the evolving professional's world, and both eyes on
the future."

—Art Kleiner, editor-in-chief, strategy+business

"Jeff Thull has changed the way we see ourselves as professionals and the value we
bring to our clients. It is hard to imagine being in this profession without Jeff's contributions. *Mastering the Complex Sale* contains the best thinking in our field."

—David L. Miller, Vice President, North American Business
    Development, Duke Corporate Education

"*Mastering the Complex Sale* is a masterpiece! It's street smart, research-backed, and
full of real-life advice on how to move all the chess pieces in the complex sales game.
You'll walk away with not only the 'what' and the 'how' of the complex sale, but also
discover how to build the mental stamina it takes to compete at the top."

—Donato J. Tramuto, CEO and Vice Chairman,
    Physicians Interactive

"Jeff Thull 'gets it'. The approach he outlines is pragmatic. *Mastering the Complex
Sale* captures the essence of how an organization must approach defining and delivering real value . . . and the benefits this provides to everyone involved in the process."

—Kristina Robinson, Vice President and General Manager,
    HP–Business Intelligence Solutions.

"Don't read this book without a highlighter and Post-its to capture the concepts
and apply them today. You can really sink your teeth into the real life examples and
scenarios. We adopted the principles that Jeff introduced in the first edition
and really increased our market share over the competition. The concept of 'value
clarity' in this edition is already enabling our sales executives and engineers to drive
even more profit going forward."

—Chris Krieps, President, Compressor Controls Corporation

"We have been leveraging Jeff's Thought Leadership for more than 20 years. As a
CEO with a global client base, I have found the Diagnostic Business Development
process to be an invaluable tool. To be successful today, CEOs must get more involved in understanding and executing their sales strategy through an integrated
organizational capability. This book is a powerful guide for building that capability
and assuring predictable and profitable growth."

—David Frigstad, Chairman, Frost & Sullivan

"In this book, Jeff does a phenomenal job of providing both sales reps and ma[n]ment a blueprint for success. It leads the way in developing innovative sales st[ra]gies and continues to be one of the most profound learning experiences methodologies. It is a proven sales method and a powerful prescription for our going success."

—Mark N. Groudas, Vice President, Americas Field Operations,
  Waters Corporation

"If you're picking this up for the first time, or want to see what's new in the secon[d] edition, either way, once you read *Mastering the Complex Sale*, there's no turnin[g] back. Jeff Thull once again provides a clear path to what works in today's realities[.] Follow it and you will succeed!"

—Ron Anson, Director of Corporate Development,
  American College of Cardiology

"Jeff Thull's approach to Diagnostic Selling has been the sales backbone of my business from selling capital equipment in the mid 80s, to executives for complex factory level solutions, where my top line went up, my margins improved, and my sales team's hit rate soared to a number one market share position. Today, as CEO, it is critical that my global sales team understands how to analyze our customers' true needs, diagnose what is really happening, design collaborative solutions, and get paid for the value we provide. This advanced *Mastering the Complex Sale* book is leading-edge and even more relevant to my business than ever before."

—Jeffrey L. Timms, President and CEO, Microscan Solutions Inc.

"*Mastering the Complex Sale* is a must-read book! Jeff Thull changes the game of selling by showing sellers how to quantify their business value step-by-step and help their customers get clarity on why they need to buy. The result—you will win more sales."

—Brian Carroll, CEO, InTouch, author of *Lead Generation for the Complex Sale*

"The biggest truth in today's business world is increased complexity. Collaboration and trust between seller and buyer are critical to navigating that complexity, and Jeff Thull is the architect and designer of just how it's done. The more buyers and sellers at all levels that read this book, the more they, and we, will all benefit."

—Charles H. Green, co-author, *The Trusted Advisor*,
  author, *Trust-based Selling*

"Jeff's insights continue to break through the traditional paradigms of selling. 'If you commoditize your customer, they will commoditize you,' should cause some very serious soul searching and Jeff's answers to this challenge, when adopted, will lead to significant success. If you are serious about not being commoditized, you need to become a master of the complex sale. Thull's recipe for success—Discover, Diagnose, Design, and Deliver—has worked extremely well for us, and I am confident his expanded perspectives in this second edition will take us to the next level."

—Ron McCullough, Vice President Sales and Marketing,
  Fives North American Combustion, Inc.

"This book is packed with pragmatic advice that is applicable across multiple industries, different cultures, and mature and developing economies. Jeff's Diagnostic Business Development process provides a clear methodology to create and capture value for our customers and develop sustainable, long-term relationships based on providing a credible source of business advantage. If you only consult one book, then this is it!"

—Gary Lord, New Business Development Leader,
   Dow Corning Healthcare Industries

"Jeff's approach to the complex sale is both accurate and insightful. Any sales organization that embraces and puts *Mastering the Complex Sale* and the models and strategies of the Prime Process into practice will have a tremendous business advantage."

—Stan Luboda, Senior Vice President SISD Sales
   and Business Development, Cognex Corporation

"Thull's clear and distinctive advice provides the reader with a real-world road map for maximizing results in high-stakes sales. Diagnostic Business Development takes today's consultative salesperson's game to the next level. This book is mandatory for those looking to gain a true competitive advantage and distinguish themselves from the competition."

—Donny Holender, Senior Vice President, The Reynolds
   and Reynolds Company

"Jeff Thull has done a brilliant job of capturing a straightforward and immensely lucrative way for executives to get a handle on your complex sales. He takes you to the heart of delivering measurable results for your customers, resulting in increased margins and customer loyalty."

—Todd C. Cozzens, Chief Executive Officer and Vice Chairman, Picis

"*Mastering the Complex Sale* lays out the most significant business and sales strategy to come along in years. It is clearly leading-edge thinking. As a technology innovator, we see it as a must. Read it and win!"

—Tim Klein, CEO, ATTO Technology, Inc.

"If you're tired of being the 'unpaid consultant' and engaging in countless 'dry runs,' Thull's *Mastering the Complex Sale* shows you how to cut through the clutter and cut to the chase. This book gives you everything you need to transition from conventional to complex sales. A real adventure!"

—Per Lofving, Senior Director, McGraw-Hill Construction

"Thull's description of self-commoditization should be a real wake-up call. There's more mileage in those few pages than most sales books have in total. Read it, apply it, and get ready to step away from your competition."

—Krishna Chettayar, Industry Solutions Executive, Acxiom Corporation

the Mastering Complex Sale

Second Edition

Mastering the Complex Sale

HOW TO COMPETE AND WIN WHEN THE STAKES ARE HIGH!

Second Edition

JEFF THULL

WILEY

John Wiley & Sons, Inc.

Published by John Wiley & Sons, Inc., Hoboken, New Jersey.
Published simultaneously in Canada.

Mastering the Complex Sale®, Diagnostic Selling®, Diagnostic Business Development®, Diagnostic Marketing®, and Prime Resource®, are registered trademarks of Prime Resource Group, Inc. Diagnostic Maps™, Key Thoughts™, and Value Life Cycle™ are trademarks of Prime Resource Group, Inc.

For general information on our other products and services or for technical support, please contact our Customer Care Department within the United States at (800) 762-2974, outside the United States at (317) 572-3993, or fax (317) 572-4002.

Wiley also publishes its books in a variety of electronic formats. Some content that appears in print may not be available in electronic books. For more information about Wiley products, visit our website at www.wiley.com.

Library of Congress Cataloging-in-Publication Data:

Thull, Jeff, 1949-
  Mastering the complex sale : how to compete and win when the stakes are
high! / Jeff Thull. – 2nd ed.
      p. cm.
  ISBN 978-0-470-53311-6 (cloth)
  e-ISBNs 978-0-470-63257-4, 978-0-470-63258-1, 978-0-470-63259-8
  1. Selling—Handbooks, manuals, etc.   2.   Relationship marketing–Handbooks,
manuals, etc.   I. Title.
  HF5438.25.T525 2010
  658.85—dc21

                                                           2009054053

Printed in the United States of America

20 19 18 17 16

Contents

Foreword

WAYNE HUTCHINSON

Vice President, Category and Supplier Management,
Shell International, The Hague, The Netherlands

When we began planning our annual sales meeting at Shell Global Solutions in 2004, we decided to recognize our top salespeople with a special rainmaker's award. We wanted to give this award to at least ten salespeople and decided that to win the award, each of them should have written at least $10 million in business in the previous year. The only problem was we didn't have ten salespeople who qualified and we had to drop the bar to $7 million. Five years later, when we started planning our 2009 sales meeting, we had 22 salespeople who had each written over $25 million worth of business the year before . . . in a *single* deal. Diagnostic Business Development®, the subject of the book you are about to read and the brainchild of its author, Jeff Thull, played an instrumental role in this feat.

Like the first edition of *Mastering the Complex Sale*, this newly updated and revised edition perfectly articulates the challenges we faced at Shell Global Solutions, challenges with which many business-to-business companies, large and small, continue to struggle. In 2003, when I arrived to head up sales and marketing, we had the most comprehensive and best set of technologies and services for plants in the oil and gas, petrochemical production, and other processing industries. We knew they were the best because they had been developed for and refined in Shell's own facilities around the world. We also had a great brand. As a unit of one of the world's leading oil and petrochemical companies, we had no problem cold calling and getting appointments with top executives in the industries we served. But once our salespeople got face-to-face with prospective customers, far too often they simply pulled out our thick catalog of 850 discrete offerings, which ranged from consulting engagements to complicated process technologies to simple widgets, and took the position of "We've got it all. What do you need?"

As Jeff explains in Chapter 1, our approach and our skills were stuck somewhere between Era 1 and Era 2, and we needed to start thinking and behaving in terms of Era 3, which is all about customer value, improving the *customer's* business. We had to rethink our portfolio of offerings from an "outside in" or customer perspective. So, we went to the 52 groups involved in the development and delivery of our 850 offerings and we asked them, one by one, to describe the value that our customers derived from using our technologies and services. The majority of their responses were solution focused and enumerated features and benefits.

We asked, "What's the business value of our anti-corrosion tool?"

"Business value? It doesn't make money. It eliminates corrosion in the processing room in a refinery or chemical plant."

"Sure, but what happens in the absence of this tool? What happens if you don't eliminate corrosion in the processing room?"

"Well, eventually there will probably be a fire or an explosion."

"If that happened, what would be the consequences—what would it cost the customer?"

The value-hypothesis lights began to flicker on.

Thinking about our portfolio in terms of customer value also led us to the realization that the bulk of the value we provided was not in the specific offering, but in our expertise in integrating them into value-added packages and delivering them to customers in specific sequences that optimized the value captured by the customer. In fact, we realized we could double the measurable value of our solutions through the proper integration and sequencing of their delivery. Previously, we had been selling our technologies and services separately, and none of our salespeople were fully conversant in all of them. Different salespeople (as well as representatives from each of our 52 delivery groups) were trying to sell different solutions to the same customers at the same time. Sometimes customers were visited three times in a single week by three different people from Shell Global Solutions. We changed our approach to dedicated sales professionals working with each customer, and they focused on selling larger, more comprehensive solutions. We were soon winning orders that were not subject to the bidding process. Because of the breadth of the solutions we could deliver, our competitors couldn't match them.

Rethinking our portfolio led us to reconsider who we were selling to and to seek out what Jeff calls the "prime customer." We didn't want to sell 850 different products and services to a million customers. We wanted to sell large, complex, multimillion dollar deals and create ongoing relationships with customers who would want to work with us on an ongoing basis. So we segmented our customers and ranked them into three levels based on the value we could deliver to them and the revenue we could earn if we served them well. Then we reassigned our sales force accordingly.

To give you a sense of the tremendous impact this major change had in how we managed our portfolio and that our customers had on our sales costs and results, consider this:

between 2004 and 2009, we reduced the size of our sales force by over 60 percent—from 110 to 42 professionals—and we increased our average contract size by 800 percent and tripled our revenues.

Of course, it took a lot more than a simple re-jiggering of how we positioned our products and services and how we ranked our customer base to achieve results like this. We needed to rethink our value-selling strategy and turn our approach to selling on its head. As you will learn in this book, you can't sell value as if it were just another product feature or benefit; customers won't believe your claims. Who can blame them, given their past experiences with the return on investment (ROI) hype and value promises made by salespeople? I knew this when I went to work for Shell Global Solutions—many sales professionals know deep down that there is something fundamentally flawed in the way they have been trained and encouraged to sell. I didn't see it put into words until the first time I read *Mastering the Complex Sale*.

It became clear that we had to stop presenting and start working with our customers to reach a shared understanding of what they were missing and how much it was costing them *before* we offered to sell anything—even if they said they were ready to buy right now. We needed a repeatable process that would enable us to analyze a customer's current situation and then look at our current portfolio of products and services and identify those that would add the most value to the customer's business. The interesting thing is, like most business-to-business companies, we already had a few highly successful salespeople who were engaging with customers in this way, but they could not tell us exactly what they did or why it worked. Jeff built a very successful business around decoding, capturing, and teaching what the best are doing. This book provides such a process—Diagnostic Business

Development—and explains why and how it works. Jeff Thull and his group helped us to transform the way we think about, structure, and execute customer engagements so completely that I don't think it's entirely accurate to call what we do "selling" anymore.

Because the way we sold changed so dramatically, we had to figure out how to get our sales force to think and behave very differently than it had in the past. In order to diagnose problems and design solutions, the sales force needed to become comfortable working at every level of the customer's organization, understand how customer perspectives on and measurements of value change with function and job descriptions, and adopt a collaborative, non-confrontational style. As you will see in the pages ahead, this style isn't part of the traditional sales profile, but it needs to be.

The new edition of *Mastering the Complex Sale* delivers a number of refinements that sales professionals at all levels, with all sizes of sales, will want to read, digest, and re-read. I would also direct the attention of sales executives and other business leaders to the chapters of Part 3, which describe the full implications of Jeff's thinking on the sales function and the entire organization. In this section, you will learn that Diagnostic Business Development isn't just a sales strategy, process, or skill set. It's an organizational capability. Sure, you can improve the results of individual salespeople by handing them this book and asking them to put the ideas it contains to work, but to really capture the full potential of Jeff's thinking, and the opportunity that lies in front of you, everybody in your company needs to think and work this way, and your internal systems need to support this approach. You've got to start thinking in organizational terms.

What most sales consultants and sales books don't mention is that superlative sales results require more than a great sales process and a highly motivated, highly skilled sales force. Jeff does not sidestep the hard truth that sustained results require a company-wide commitment and effort. Your sales force needs an entire organization that supports its efforts. It needs products and services that are capable of delivering real and measurable customer value. It needs marketing initiatives and collateral that will help customers recognize when and how their performance is at risk from the absence of that value, as opposed to the "latest and greatest" focus of value messaging. It needs sales managers who can help the sales force continue to improve its diagnostic and interpersonal skills, hold its feet to the fire when necessary, and run interference when it bumps up against the inevitable internal constraints. Finally, the sales force needs a service organization that can ensure that customers actually capture the value they have invested in and help to identify as-yet-unrealized value that can lead to additional value creation capabilities for your customers.

We've worked hard to embed Diagnostic Business Development into Shell Global Solutions' corporate DNA. Everyone in the company knows the diagnostic approach and communication principles that Jeff describes in this book, and I could have a conversation with anyone here about Diagnostic Selling®. I was actually surprised at how quickly our engineers embraced this style of communication. They became very interested as soon as they realized that how they talk to other people— colleagues as well as customers—can either open up or shut down communication.

Our marketing team is now working hand-in-hand with sales. We've culled a forest of sales collateral down to about twenty brochures that are focused on the symptoms customers experience when value is not being applied. Our case studies had been 80 percent focused on solution and 20 percent on the problem being solved. Today, we've almost completely reversed that emphasis. Our web site was redesigned in the same way. You can view it at www.shell.com/views/business.html, upon selecting "Global Solutions."

To be sure that the marketing team understood how to support our new selling strategy, we gave it the same training as the sales force, adding the Diagnostic Marketing® program that helps marketing provision the sales organization to approach the customer in a diagnostic manner. Now when sales asks for marketing support, our marketers use their diagnostic skills to design events and materials that produce the maximum value for both salespeople and customers. Marketing also reconsidered the Shell Global Solutions brand. We eliminated discussions about specific technologies and services in our brand-building campaigns. Now we are positioned as partners who work with customers to create value in their businesses.

In terms of delivering the value we sell, our service teams are engaging in a diagnostic way with customers to ensure that they get what they need from a value perspective. Our delivery groups are thinking in terms of measured customer value now. Customers often try to change the scope of a project once it's sold for reasons that are unconnected to the actual value they could achieve. Our teams now know that if they don't deliver demonstrable value, the customer will not continue to do business with us and eventually we are going to run out of customers. Instead, they continue to diagnose and clarify the value and get the project back on track.

We can turn on a dime to define value from our customer's perspective and be able to connect it to their current business drivers. In this challenging market, when so many of our customers are struggling to control costs, our engineers have been reconfiguring our portfolio into industry-leading suites of cost-reduction technologies and services.

Following our success in Shell Global Solutions, we were asked to create a tailored version of the Diagnostic program for the top commercial deal leaders within Shell. These are the individuals who are orchestrating mergers, acquisitions, licensing rights, joint ventures, and so on, and these deals can run into the billions of dollars and with agreements that can surpass forty years. These individuals can be selling in one part of the deal and buying in another part of the deal. When we think about "mastering the complex sale," we think of it as "mastering a complex value exchange." Hopefully, you are starting to see that the greatest use of this book is as a guide to building a Diagnostic Business Development capability in your company. Anything less and you will be leaving money on the table.

If everything I've written thus far hasn't convinced you that *Mastering the Complex Sale* has the potential to transform your personal and your company's business results, here's one last thing that I'll ask you to consider: I've recently been reassigned to work in Shell International's contracting and procurement function with Shell's twenty top suppliers, who together represent around $60 billion in annual spending. Why this position? Because we believe that the way companies typically buy has the potential to strip more value than costs from their organizations, and if we teach and allow our suppliers to sell to us in the same way that Shell Global Solutions has been selling to its customers, we will be able to co-create the optimal amount of value for all parties in our value chain. Our pilot project has strongly confirmed that belief.

When you really take a closer look, your very best salespeople do not "sell" in a conventional sense and your very best customers do not "buy" in a conventional sense. They collaborate in a quality and transparent decision process with the objective to optimize the value for all parties. Jeff Thull has unlocked the code on the best way to do business. I know you'll enjoy the read, and, most certainly your results, as you apply Diagnostic Business Development!

Acknowledgments

Looking back on 40-plus years of business, which includes 28 years since founding Prime Resource Group, I undoubtedly have many individuals to thank for their contributions and support. I first thank my lifetime partner in marriage and five businesses, Pat Thull. I realize the concept of being partners in marriage and in business intrigues many, enviable to quite a few, and is unimaginable to others. I can describe our partnership only as "as good as it gets." Pat has been an integral and driving force behind the growth of our organization and the development of the Prime Process. She is a student of the process and a master of the complex sale. She has brought in and served multiple clients in her role as vice president of sales and marketing and now COO of Prime Resource Group. Her editorial contribution has had a significant impact on the clarity of this book.

I thank my parents, who instilled in me an attitude of accomplishment, and continually encouraged and supported my earliest entrepreneurial pursuits. My father provided a role model that I found reflected repeatedly in many successful sales professionals I have met. He sold industrial building granite for 35 years and sold to executives of some of the most admired corporations in America and through some of the most well-known architects in this country. I have a vivid memory of taking a business trip with him when I was 12 years old. I witnessed the respect he had for his clients and the reciprocal respect they showed him. I was immediately struck with the greatness of his profession. I am most grateful that both my parents lived to see the beginnings of Diagnostic Business Development and the success of Prime Resource Group.

The list of clients and associates that have contributed to the evolution of this process is long, starting with my first sales manager, Al Miller, and my first business mentor, Bob New. Two valued clients were Ken Bozevich and Lovell Baker, 3M managers, who took a calculated risk on a "radical" new sales program and a young consultant some 27 years ago. I thank Al Eggert, Ben Michelson, and Dave Madsen, of 3M HIS, who built and supported one of the first and most successful implementations of the Prime Process. As of this writing, we are continuing to serve 3M HIS at a significant level. I am very proud about the power and longevity of the process and the long-term client relationships we enjoy. I am grateful also to Peter Muldowney, Terry Slattery, Bob Groening, Don Beveridge, Bill Graham, Nido Qubein, Rob Castien, Bob Brockman, Richard Brooks, Per Lofving, Ilan Shanon, Charlie Morris, Mario Concha, Robin Wolfson, and John Willig. You will read Wayne Hutchinson's experience with Mastering the Complex Sale® in his foreword. I am very grateful to him and Greg Lewin, who made a significant effort to build the diagnostic capability into their entire organization. It is one thing for us as consultants to analyze, advise, and teach this process—it is quite another to provide the leadership and resources to achieve the personal and organizational value this system has to offer.

The early development of this material began with the creation of our Diagnostic Selling program in 1985 and was assisted by a gifted editor and writer, Tom Watson. John Sullivan, PhD, and Judy Robinson, PhD, have provided invaluable support with their expertise in instructional de-sign and curriculum development to capture the Diagnostic Business Development Process and turn it into a replicable process that has been embraced across multiple industries and cultures.

We began this project knowing I would need serious adult supervision to keep on track and sift through moun-tains of information, research, and experiences to distill a topic as broad as Mastering the Complex Sale into a single book. We thank Ted and Donna Kinni for doing just that. Their expert assistance in crafting our story initially and now helping us with this revision has been impressive and enjoyable. Thank you to the entire team at John Wiley & Sons, Inc., including Matt Holt, who took the initial risk on the first edition, and Dan Ambrosio, our editor, who has guided this revised edition.

A special thank you goes to Jennifer, Jessica, and Brian.

Introduction to the Second Edition

Value remains the most sought after and least understood factor in the world of complex sales. Companies continue to invest in high-value solutions designed to solve their customers' problems, fuel profitable growth, and set them apart from their competitors. They also continue to struggle with the pressures of complexity and commoditization, which have escalated since I wrote the first edition of *Mastering the Complex Sale*, and while I work with business-to-business companies around the world.

Their challenges in today's volatile markets—and the focus of my work—can be summarized in two words: *value clarity*. Companies are finding it increasingly difficult to defend their value in the marketplace because it is increasingly difficult to connect that value to customers' situations and quantify it. The more complex customers' situations and the solutions that can address them are, the more uncertain customers become. This uncertainty manifests in decision paralysis: The percentage of sales opportunities ending in no decision at all is running well above 35 percent for most business-to-business sellers. The consequences of this dismal reality include lost revenues, long sales cycles, and unpredictable outcomes. Customer uncertainty is consuming an alarmingly high percentage of company resources.

To put it bluntly, because business-to-business sellers are unable to provide their customers with value clarity, they cannot defend their value. As a result, they have no alternative but to cut prices, which requires cutting costs to maintain margins. This can lead to a very dangerous downward spiral, in which the organic growth and profits required to sustain their businesses spin further and further out of their reach.

Value clarity defeats uncertainty, and this book is designed to equip you with the organizational capability needed to create value clarity and decisiveness both within your company and on the part of your customers.

I remain convinced that Diagnostic Business Development® is the best way to create, connect, quantify, and deliver customer value in the current era. Conventional sales approaches, which were designed for simpler times and transactions, cannot manage the escalation in complexity, customer requirements, commoditization, and competition that sales professionals everywhere are facing. Certainly, doing more of something that isn't working in the first place isn't the way to compete more effectively and win more sales.

Business-to-business companies need a smarter way to bring their value to market and transform it into profitable growth. They need a platform that is specifically designed for the complex sales arena, one that offers a system and the skills and the mental discipline needed to execute it. Diagnostic Business Development is this smarter way to sell because it converts the conventional solutions-based, seller-first approach into a diagnostic, customer-first approach. It eliminates obsolete sales processes driven by premature presentations, debate, and confrontation, and replaces them with a step-by-step process of mutual confirmation between the sales team and the customer. It transforms the customer's stereotypical impression of salespeople as predators into one in which salespeople are seen as valued business partners who bring credibility, integrity, and dependability to the business relationship.

In short, Diagnostic Business Development is a smarter way to sell because it enables sales professionals to *stop selling* in the conventional sense. Instead, the sales engagement becomes a guided decision process in which salespeople work with customers to Discover, Diagnose, Design, and Deliver the highest-value solution to their problems. Diagnostic Business Development enables us to:

- Get beyond selling to managing decisions. All good salespeople have a sales process and all customers have a buying process. The problem is that they invariably have conflicting objectives that create an adversarial relationship. We need to set aside confrontational processes and replace them with a collaborative decision process, provided by the sales professional.

- Get beyond problem solving to facilitating change. Providing quality solutions to customer problems no longer ensures a successful sale and certainly does not guarantee a successful implementation. Change, along with all the attendant risks involved, is the key issue that customers face. We need to help them understand, prepare for, and navigate the change required to ensure the successful implementation of our solutions, achieve the value they are expecting, and measure the value they have achieved.

- Get beyond meeting needs to managing expectations. Just because we see a need does not mean that our customers see it or understand it as clearly as we do and will do something about it. We need to clarify our value by connecting it to our customers' performance metrics and quantify our value impact with a number our customers believe. Further, we must clarify our customers' expectations about solutions in a manner that brings them the confidence to invest in our solutions.

- Get beyond transactions to managing relationships. In the rush to close deals, we too often forget the human factor and squander the long-term opportunity. We need to address the hopes, fears, and aspirations of our customers and create mutually beneficial relationships.

- Get beyond rote talking points and "value messages" to rich, interactive conversations. Too often, we react to customers with fixed responses, without asking for clarification or deeper thinking. As a result, we sound just like every other salesperson. We need to communicate at a level that fosters a crystal-clear, mutual understanding of our customers' challenges and objectives in order to provide them with the best solutions.

It struck me, as I began working on this new edition, how much the Diagnostic Business Development platform has evolved since the first edition. Since then, I've written two additional books. *The Prime Solution* is a strategic view written for senior leadership teams who want to understand how Diagnostic Business Development can be used to bridge the *value gap* that exists between them and their customers. *Exceptional Selling* is a practical guide to the art and craft of diagnostic conversations written for sales professionals who are seeking to become valued business advisors to their customers. Both projects have enabled me to expand and refine the ideas in this book.

My clients have also stimulated my thinking and I'm very grateful to them for it. We continue to teach and support the implementation of Diagnostic Business Development on a global stage, and it is fascinating to see how the talented executives and sales professionals in these companies have extended and adapted the ideas in this book to fit their unique situations. Because of all of this, this edition of

Mastering the Complex Sale contains a great deal of new and street-tested information.

We've developed powerful approaches to value clarity during the past few years and they play a much more central role in this edition. I first formulated the *Value Life Cycle*™ concept in my second book, and now it is expanded and woven into the Diagnostic Business Development platform. As a result, you will be able to help your customers clarify, connect, and quantify value in a manner that will clearly set you apart from your competition.

Individual sales professionals can read this book and use it to improve their results exponentially, but it has far greater potential when developed as a capability by sales organizations and their companies. Implementing Diagnostic Business Development in an integrated manner in the sales organization can raise the performance level in a significant percentage of the sales force. Better yet, as evidenced by clients of my firm, companies that embed Diagnostic Business Development as an organizational *capability* can optimize their value chains, creating a value-driven company in the process. Wayne Hutchinson's foreword, with its description of Shell Global Solutions' success, provides a clear picture of the results you can achieve if you decide to build a Diagnostic Business Development capability across your entire business.

Finally, this new edition contains myriad refinements and additions to the Diagnostic Business Development platform that will provide first-time readers with a more comprehensive introduction. It will also provide a richer, more nuanced understanding to the tens of thousands of you who made the first edition of *Mastering the Complex Sale* the leading sales strategy book of the past decade. In fact, many of the changes in this new edition were stimulated by the questions you asked and the comments you made in our consulting engagements and seminars.

On that note, I'd like to thank every sales professional and executive who contributed to this book—from new recruits wondering how to best frame that first call, to the sales veterans who are fine-tuning their diagnostic skills; from the line managers who are working hard to meet and beat their targets, to senior executives who are trying to convert customer value to profitable growth. You are the primary motivation behind this book and almost 30 years of work focused on mastering the complex sale. Enjoy the read! Enjoy your journey!

Mastering
the
Complex Sale

Second Edition

The World in Which We Sell

Caught between Complexity and Commoditization

If Our Solution Is So Complex, Why Is It Treated as a Commodity?

The frustration triggered by this chapter's title is shared by a large number of executives, marketers, and sales professionals who are taking their complex, high-value solutions to market and finding it increasingly difficult to win profitable sales. Ironically, it is also shared by their customers, who are wrestling with mission-critical decisions, evaluating solutions that all sound the same, and struggling to achieve the value they expect, when experience has shown them that far too many solutions come packaged with a high degree of risk and a low probability of success. This phenomenon places all of us clearly in the third era of sales.

This is an era in which customers are not saying, "I need a solution!" They know they can get comparable solutions from credible sources. Instead, they are saying, "I need help!"

> *"I need help in making multiple decisions around this purchase."*
>
> *"I need help in quantifying the business impact of this project to make sure it is the best use of my resources."*
>
> *"I need help in getting my organization to align around the implementation and make the changes required to optimize the value of your solution."*
>
> *"I need help to show measurable results."*

Are you equipped to help your customers in Era 3? It seems, at first glance, like a strange question, but it's essential that it be examined more closely. The question is valid because most businesses are applying sales strategies, processes, collateral, and skills originally designed for a world that no longer exists.

John Sullivan, my colleague and director of professional services for Prime Resource Group, wrote about the three eras of selling in the foreword to the first edition of this book.[1] He described the Era 1 approach with its focus on cold calling, presenting, and closing, and a strong dose of overcoming objections. Salespeople were taught to be persuaders (some would call them pests). I like to describe it as the age of "show and tell," "spray and pray," "cram and jam," and "grab 'em by the tie and choke 'em 'til they buy." Salespeople didn't ask customers many questions at all; they told them what to do and they did it in a very aggressive manner. These Era 1 tactics are the source of the common sales stereotypes that live in the minds of many people today. They provided the major impetus behind the creation of procurement systems designed to counteract aggressive sales tactics and protect customers from buying the wrong thing or paying inflated prices.

The sales profession worked to redeem itself with the Era 2 sales approaches that were first articulated by sales gurus like Larry Wilson with his concept of "counselor selling," and Mack Hanan, whose book *Consultative Selling* was first published in 1970 and is still in print seven editions later. They suggested that salespeople ask questions to learn the customer's view of his or her problem and what the customer thinks the solution should be. Then, salespeople would tailor their products and services to match that picture. In Era 2, salespeople received some new tools and skills, were taught how to do needs analysis (I ask you what you need), and received listening training (so I actually pay attention to what you tell me). There was a lot of relationship skill building, too, because counselors and consultants needed to be seen as credible and trustworthy. Salespeople morphed from persuaders into consultants. It was the era that positioned the salesperson as a problem solver.

You're probably thinking, "What's not to like about Era 2? Why do we need an updated sales approach at all?" The answer is you might not. There is a very subtle assumption underlying all of the great Era 2 sales processes, and if it still holds true for you, they will continue to serve you well. If not, and you find what has worked well for you is no longer effective, your customer may be in Era 3, and your Era 2 strategy and approach could be sabotaging your efforts.

The hidden assumption of Era 2 is that customers clearly understand the problems they need to solve and the solutions that are required to solve them. This was usually true when the Era 2 sales paradigm was formulated. But it is a deadly assumption that may no longer be valid for your customers—and it isn't for a vast majority of today's complex sales. Therefore, if the assumption is no longer valid, the Era 2 paradigm is no longer effective. An Era 2 salesperson engaging with an Era 3 customer is like a doctor who allows patients to self-diagnose their illnesses and self-prescribe medications. In the sales profession, as in the medical world, it is reckless and harmful behavior and a formula for failure.

A question that we like to pose in our seminars is, "What if a doctor conducted annual physicals using the strategy and approach of an Era 2 salesperson?" My physical would go something like this:

> *Doc says, "Hi Jeff, how are you doing today?" I say, "Great, just great." Doc says, "Are there any concerns I could help you with, anything keeping you awake at night?" To which I respond, "Well, actually, there is. I'm getting to the age where I've noticed a few of my contemporaries have been having heart problems. One, a friend, seemingly in top shape, a guy who exercised much more than me, had a massive heart attack and was gone in an instant. Just tragic. I am really concerned that something like that could*

happen to me. Is there anything that you could do to prevent that from happening?" Doc says, "Why certainly, Jeff. It's likely that clogged arteries caused his heart attack and we could help you with that. Tell me, were you thinking about open heart, bypass surgery, or angioplasty?"

I'm not sure if you're chuckling at the idea of a physician taking direction from an unqualified patient, but in a live workshop, this elicits a lot of laughter. Let's continue my exam and see where this takes us.

I feel compelled to answer the doctor—and I do know something about this complex area, so I reply, "Well, Doctor, I think open heart would be a little too messy and painful, and I don't want to be out of work for a long time. I'd be more interested in the angioplasty." "Not a problem," says the doctor. "Let me tell you about these great coated stents that I could use . . ."

This story is laughable, but if you listen to the questions that salespeople ask in an Era 2 approach, you will quickly see that they are essentially asking customers to do a self-diagnosis and self-prescription and report back the results. Typical questions of Era 2:

What concerns do you have?
What's keeping you awake at night?
What are some of the major causes of your problems?
What are the consequences of your problems?
Who besides you will be involved in the decision?
What are you looking for in a solution?
What sort of budget have you set aside?

The problem with the previous list of questions is that if your customer, like the patient, is not experienced or knowledgeable enough to self-diagnose and self-prescribe, you are basing your proposal and betting the sale on incomplete and often inaccurate information. Even worse, your competitors are likely asking the same questions that you are, so everything that you tell the customer based on this flawed information sounds exactly like what they will be telling the customer. It's a perfect setup for self-commoditization.

So, if your customers have difficulty understanding and quantifying the impact of the problems you solve, and they have difficulty sorting through and understanding the competing solutions, they are squarely in Era 3. The problem is that most companies and their sales and marketing strategies have not evolved with the times. A disturbingly large number of sales forces are still selling in Era 1, and the vast majority are embracing the Era 2 approach. These sales forces are being squeezed between two opposing forces: increasing complexity and rapid commoditization (see Figure 1.1).

The Driving Force of Complexity

The defining characteristic of Era 3 is that our customers' problems and our solutions to them are becoming increasingly complex. Much of this complexity is emerging from the changing nature of business itself.

The structure of organizations is becoming more complex. In many cases, decentralized and lean organizational structures have replaced fixed, hierarchical infrastructures. In the process, decision-making powers have often migrated from the technical, clinical, and operational levels to purchasing departments and professional managers who frequently consider buying decisions from only the vital, but nonetheless limited, financial perspective of acquisition

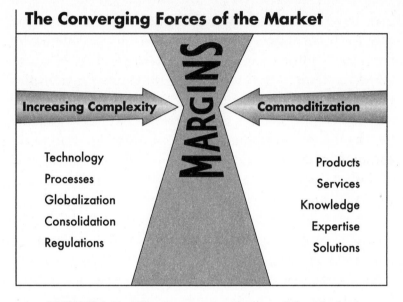

FIGURE 1.1   The Converging Forces of the Market

cost. Over the past few years, we have also seen approval levels migrate higher in the organization, and now, more than ever, the ability to gain access to and engage and interact with the executive is not optional. As a result, salespeople are finding it increasingly difficult to understand and navigate through their customers' companies. Identifying the centers of decision and influence in today's corporate labyrinths is quite complicated and constrained, and with increasing frequency, customers themselves cannot define or even understand their own decision processes.

Globalization is also exacerbating the growing complexity of organizational structure. Today, sales and marketing professionals are often engaging with companies that encompass many different languages and unique cultures. "Where in the world are the decision makers?" is not a rhetorical question in an increasing number of situations.

The restructuring of organizations has extended up and down the supply chain. Customers are consolidating, fewer companies are controlling higher percentages of demand, and fewer competitors are controlling higher percentages of supply. In addition, the speed with which these transformations are occurring is unprecedented. Witness the chaos and upheaval in sectors such as financial services, automotive, construction, and airlines which is ongoing as of this writing.

At the same time, buyers are demanding more attention and a closer relationship with those suppliers whom they choose to give their business. They are drastically reducing their supply bases and asking the remaining suppliers to take a more active role in their business processes, to become business partners, and open their books and operations in the quest to create value on both sides of the relationship. They are asking their suppliers to add value at much deeper levels than has typically been delivered, and to prove it by tracking progress, measuring the value delivered and achieved, and proving the return on investment. This is adding complexity to the seller's process. As a result, buying decisions include more considerations and more players, and those players are often located at higher levels in the organization.

There is an even more sobering consideration here: If your customers are tightening up their supply chains, there will be fewer sales opportunities. Further, one lost sale in the chain could easily translate into the long-term loss of the customer. Era 3 is increasingly becoming an environment in which the winners of deals take a substantial share, if not all of the market, and the losers are left out in the cold.

Your customers are facing similar challenges. They are under constant pressure to do more with less and advance their products and services. Companies tend not to see the world clearly through their customers' eyes, but when they do, they find that they face many of the same problems. Their customers' business environments are more competitive than ever, technological advances are radically altering their industries and markets, and their margin for error is always shrinking. The increased complexity of their environment translates directly to increased complexity in the problems they need to solve.

The solutions that we design to address those problems are correspondingly complex. Our solutions need to incorporate complex technical innovations and address challenges that are constantly surfacing in a fast-changing business world. Along with our customers, our margins for error are shrinking as well.

Finally, complexity is driven by competition. To stay on top of our markets, we often find ourselves trapped in "innovation races" with our competitors, and constantly adding features to our solutions. In doing so, we can actually outrun the needs and the comprehension of our customers. Harvard Business School professor Clayton Christensen calls this "performance oversupply," and says, "In their efforts to stay ahead by developing competitively superior products, many companies don't realize the speed at which they are moving up-market, over-satisfying the needs of their original customers as they race the competition toward higher-performance, higher-margin markets."[2] This race is a major contributor to the long lists of new product features that salespeople present to their customers, even though they often add very little incremental value, almost always create confusion, and often cause the customer to drop into decision paralysis.

In short, the entire business-to-business sector continues to escalate in complexity. This trend gives rise to the second driving force of Era 3—commoditization.

The Driving Force of Commoditization

Commoditization is a big word for a phenomenon that salespeople face every day in Era 3—that is, price pressure. Customers are constantly devaluing the unique and differentiating solutions you bring to your market and trying to reduce their buying decision to the lowest common denominator—the selling price. The pressure to treat all offerings in a category of products and services as identical in value arises in some instances from very real conditions, and in others from the customer's personal demands and emotional needs. In either case, the pressure exists and sales professionals must deal with it.

The emergence of new technology is stimulating commoditization. A vivid example of how a technology can commoditize a product is the advancement of electronic commerce. Before the Internet, enterprise-level computer sales were considered complex sales, and all of the major computer manufacturers had large field sales organizations dedicated to that task. Today, many of those sales positions have been eliminated. Computer manufacturers still maintain sales forces for their high-volume customers, but buying any number of computers for a company can also be accomplished in a self-service, commodity-based transaction.

Even a short visit to a web site such as Dell.com makes the point crystal clear. Dell Computer Corporation was founded on a direct-to-the-customer model that eliminated the external sales and distribution chains that other PC manufacturers depended on. When e-commerce technology appeared, Dell was the first to move online. Starting in 1996, Dell customers who wanted a self-serve transaction could research, configure, and price their PCs, associated hardware, and off-the-shelf software on Dell's web site.

Dell profited handsomely from its use of the Internet as a sales and distribution channel. Unfortunately for Dell, the market caught up, and today PCs can be purchased online from all of Dell's major competitors, prices and specifications can be compared, and purchases can be made without ever speaking to a salesperson. What was once solely considered a complex product and sale has been transformed by technology (as well as customer experience and knowledge) into a commoditized product and sale. Now Dell is experimenting with sales and distribution models that offer higher levels of service in an attempt to differentiate itself in the marketplace. As I write this today, Dell has acquired Perot Data Systems, a professional services company that will allow it to compete with IBM and HP, both of whom have moved significantly up the value chain from hardware sales.

The second cause of commoditization is the lack of clear differentiation between competing products in the marketplace. The growing similarity between the products and services that compete in specific market niches is not a figment of customers' imaginations. When there is no difference among products, incremental value does not exist.

Consider the PC once again. Corporate buyers often see little difference between one company's PCs and the PCs of its major competitors. Who can blame them? Perhaps the logo on the box is different, but the main components of the computer—the processors, memory, disk drives, and motherboards—are often identical. Therefore, buyers are unable to discern unique value and they treat all PCs as the same, purchasing them based on price alone.

Contributing to the similarity between competing products and services are industry response times. Unless products and services are protected by law (as in the case of new prescription drugs), the length of time that their inventors or licensees enjoy the advantage of being first into the market is getting shorter and shorter. Competitors see a successful or improved product in the market and quickly match or exceed it.

Another reason it is getting more difficult to differentiate products and services is that the buyer doesn't want to differentiate them. The more complex products and services are, the harder it is for customers to compare and evaluate them. Analyzing and deciding between long lists of non-identical features can be very difficult and time consuming, but simply comparing purchase prices is much easier. This points us to the third cause of commoditization—the customer.

Customers, especially purchasing departments, who are incentivized to drive down the price of goods and services, are always trying to level the playing field. They attempt to reduce complex and valuable solutions to their lowest common denominators for good reasons. When customers are able to convince suppliers that their offerings are essentially the same, they exert tremendous downward pressure on the price. For instance, if General Electric's jet engines are the same price as Rolls Royce's jet engines, and the customer can't or won't see any difference between the two, what must be done to win the sale? Unfortunately, the easiest path, and the one that takes the least skill to execute, is to cut the price, which is why so much margin erosion occurs at the point of sale. We've seen many businesses that have chosen such a path eventually fail.

An example of the extreme impact that even the threat of commoditization can produce involves a company whose leadership team called me after its business had taken a devastating hit. This company's technology became a standard in the chip manufacturing industry. It produced highly specialized capital equipment, sold about 300 units per year, and enjoyed a very large market share. When a competitor entered the marketplace offering the "same thing" for 32 percent less, customers used this premise to pressure the original manufacturer to lower its prices. Even though the company had a very valuable solution that was superior to the competitor's, it was unable to connect and quantify that value in terms of the customer's business and the company ultimately lowered its price. This was a clear example of an outdated sales process that couldn't make it in an Era 3 world. The company dropped the average selling price of its equipment by 30 percent during the following year, a move that cost $24 million. The irony of the story is that the upstart competitor was able to build only 15 units that year, which represented a 5 percent market share. If the original manufacturer had held its prices and even lost all 15 sales, it would have been about $20 million better off overall.

What is interesting, or should I say tragic, is the strategy of "we can give you the same thing as the high-value supplier for 32 percent less,"—it is probably one of the most feeble, yet most successful, sales premises. It only works because the customer cannot discern whether the solutions are "the same thing," and the seller of the more expensive solution cannot clarify and defend its higher value.

Customers also try to commoditize complex transactions for emotional reasons. Often they are in denial about the extent of their problems. Think in personal terms: If your stomach burns and you chew an off-the-shelf antacid and you feel better, you believe your problem was minor and easily solved. If you go to your doctor who discovers you have an ulcer, an increased level of clarity and fear is reached and your problem jumps to an entirely different level.

Fear drives customers to try to commoditize transactions. It is human nature to find it difficult to admit when we don't understand problems and/or solutions or admit to concerns about making changes in our current situations. Our customers are facing many different risks, whether they change or not. They are unclear about these risks and hesitate to open up. They are often concerned about appearing less than competent in front of us, their bosses, or their peers. As a result, when customers don't understand something we tell them, they often simply nod and proceed to reduce the transaction to what they do understand—the purchase price.

Finally, there is the emotional issue of control. We must recognize the negative stereotype of a professional salesperson that exists in many customers' minds. Customers are fearful that by acknowledging complexity and admitting their own lack of understanding, they will lose control of the transaction and open themselves to manipulative sales techniques. The simpler that customers can make a sale, the less they must depend on salespeople to help them. Commoditization, in this sense, is a way for customers to maintain control of the transaction and protect themselves.

The net effect of all these causes of commoditization is the deadly spiral of shrinking profit margins.

Commoditization Is a Choice

In Era 3, business-to-business sellers are desperately seeking competitive differentiation through increasingly sophisticated products and services. Meanwhile, their customers, working in a perpetual haze of confusion and performance pressure, are treating all solutions like commodities. This leaves your company with a critical choice—whether to embrace a core strategy that supports a price-focused sale or one that supports a high-value solution.

Companies that choose the first alternative embrace the commodity sale as Dell did, as well as other companies, such as steelmaker Nucor, which in the late 1960s created an innovative mini-mill that enabled it to produce and sell steel at prices that Big Steel couldn't come close to matching. With a commodity, the total transaction cost, including price, is the differentiating factor in the marketplace. As commoditization occurs, sales skills become less and less relevant, and transactional efficiency becomes the critical edge. The professional sales force itself soon becomes a luxury that is too expensive to maintain. If your company has chosen to embrace commoditization as a dedicated strategy, reading this book is unnecessary. Instead, you should be aggressively pursuing the lowest cost structure and lowest selling price in your industry.

Embracing the commodity sale is a dangerous strategy. If your company chooses it, it is limiting its opportunities and may very well stifle its long-term potential. You need to constantly reduce your costs and prices, usually pursuing volume in order to operate successfully on razor-thin margins. Often you must simplify your value propositions to generate this volume, which reduces your power to differentiate your offerings and opens the market to new competitors. Sooner or later there is always some new company, like Dell or Nucor, which will figure out a way to do whatever it is you do cheaper than you can.

A commodity sale should only exist because the seller consciously chooses it as a strategy. The other alternative that companies can choose—I believe it's the only viable alternative for the vast majority of companies in Era 3— is to embrace the high-value strategy to fuel profitable growth. This doesn't mean that the pressure of commoditization will disappear. You will still have to cope with it and execute against it. Companies can only achieve this if their organizations are aligned to deliver on the value promise and their sales forces can clarify, connect, and quantify that value for customers. When this is done successfully, the high-value strategy becomes a sustainable competitive advantage and the pressures of commoditization recede.

In such a strategy, the differentiating factors are all the facets of value that a particular customer can realize from your solutions. Of course, the customer's total cost remains an integral element in the overall value, but only when weighed against two other elements—the savings and/or the revenue that your solutions can generate for the customer's company. I refer to this as the total value of ownership or TVO. It is a significant advance beyond the total cost of ownership or TCO. TCO, as I will detail in Chapter 5, is a limited concept; TVO provides a more holistic view of value.

I personally believe there is no such thing as a commodity. Any product or service, even sand, can be turned into a high-value solution. Back in the 1980s, Rhône-Poulenc transformed the selling of industrial sand or silica, a money-losing commodity, into a high-value solution. Silica was used in the production of tires, and the company introduced a new product—highly dispersible silica—that reduced a tire's rolling resistance enough to create a 9 percent rise in fuel efficiency. The company was able to sell this added value to its customers in the tire industry at a 75 percent premium to its competitors' products.[3]

What we need to always remember, however, is that a defining characteristic of Era 3 is that our customers cannot recognize our high-value solutions without our help. Every high-value seller must provide its customers with the means to comprehend and measure the value it provides. Sellers who don't do this will find themselves defenseless in the face of price competition.

To embrace the high-value strategy and prosper in Era 3, companies need to recruit, develop, and equip sales and marketing professionals who can create value clarity for their customers. These professionals must provide incontrovertible evidence of the risks their customers face without their solutions. I call this the "absence of value." It is similar to the "absence of health" or a "health risk." During your annual physical, your doctor is providing you with the evidence needed to support his diagnosis and recommendations.

In Era 3, successful salespeople must diagnose their customers' situations and find evidence of the absence of value, go on to quantify the financial impact of that missing value, and connect the value impact of their solutions to the performance metrics of customers and the customers they serve. This includes understanding the complex situations their customers face, configuring the complex solutions offered by their companies, and managing the complex relationships that are required to bring them both together. In short, Era 3 professionals are constantly challenged to create and clarify value for their customers and for their employers.

We see the dynamics of this complex sale challenge every day. My colleagues and I spend thousands of hours each year working with executives on developing their high-value strategies, and teaching their sales and market-ing professionals how to position and execute those strate-gies. We meet highly successful professionals who sell value-laden solutions in a wide range of industries such as software, medical devices and equipment, professional and financial services, information technology, industrial chem-icals, and manufacturing systems. The individual sales they manage produce revenues for their companies that range from tens of thousands of dollars to tens of billions of dollars. These professionals are highly educated, very sophisticated, definitely street-smart, and well paid. They are levels above the stereotypical image of salespeople that is imprinted on the public imagination, and being com-moditized is not part of their DNA.

Even though these professionals are masters of their craft, we regularly hear them express their frustration about the disconnect between their sales efforts and their results. Their most common lament is one that we've labeled the *Dry Run*. The generic version goes like this:

> *A prospective customer contacts your company with a problem that your solutions are expressly designed to address. A salesperson or team is assigned to the account. The customer is qualified, appointments are set, and your sales team interviews the customer's team to determine what they want, what their requirements are, and what they plan to invest. A well-crafted multimedia presentation is created, a complete solution within the customer's budget is proposed, and all of the customer's questions are answered. Everyone on the customer's side of the table smiles and nods at the conclusion of the formal presentation. "Yes, everything makes good business sense," says their senior executive. "Yes, your solution seems to fill our needs as we described them." You believe that the sale is in the bag, but the decision to move forward never comes. The result after weeks, months, and sometimes years of work: no decision, no sale.*

In the *Dry Run*, the customer doesn't buy from your company. The worst-case scenario ends in what we refer to as "unpaid consulting." The customer takes your solution design, shops it down the street, and buys from a competitor—or does the work that you proposed on their own. Nearly as bad is the "no-decision" scenario, in which the customer company simply doesn't take any action on a solution that for some reason you thought it needed and could afford. Based on what sales professionals tell us in surveys and interviews, it appears that 40 to 60 percent of all *Dry Runs* end in no decision at all, and that this percentage has been growing over time. Neither *Dry Run* scenario is desirable, but the no-decision result raises serious questions, such as whether the opportunity actually existed in the first place and why it was pursued at such length and cost. When we work with clients who are experiencing a significant number of no-decisions, we typically discover that there are fundamental flaws in their sales processes and execution.

Dry Runs are indicative of a complex sales environment in which outcomes are becoming increasingly random and unpredictable. We have already hinted at some of the reasons behind this, but to truly understand the situation, it is important to understand the dynamics at work within complex sales that impact customer decision making and your ability to effectively orchestrate it.

The Missing Ingredient: Professional Guidance

A complex sale is not a physical attribute of a product or a service. As we've already seen, buying sand can be a complex sale. Conversely, purchasing a highly sophisticated medical device, such as an MRI scanner, can be oversimplified and treated as a commodity sale. Nor are complex sales defined by their size. Complex sales are defined by the customer's need for outside expertise and guidance to make a quality buying decision.

Some complex sales are so massive that they reshape the dynamics within an industry. In the first edition of this book, I described the $200-billion defense contract that Lockheed Martin won in 2001 to design and manufacture the U.S. Defense Department's Joint Strike Fighter (JSF). Because the winner of the contract essentially became the nation's only fighter jet manufacturer, the now-retired Lockheed aeronautics executive James Blackwell called it "the mother of all procurements." He suggested that the JSF contract would eventually be valued at $1 trillion.[4]

The JSF contract may very well be a once-in-a-lifetime sale, but huge complex deals are commonplace in some sectors. In the energy business, for example, global oil companies regularly compete for contracts to develop the natural resources of nations. These contracts run for decades and can be worth hundreds of millions to billions of dollars annually to the companies that win them. Winning them requires connecting and quantifying value at many, many levels with myriad decision makers and influencers throughout a nation's public and private sectors. It involves extended sales teams that can quickly grow to include hundreds of people from within a company and a host of business partners. These contracts have a sales cycle that is typically counted in years, and the cost of the sale can add up to tens of millions of dollars and sometimes hundreds of millions of dollars.

The contracts associated with the development of Qatar's giant North Field, the largest non-associated natural gas field in the world with 900 trillion cubic feet of proven reserves, are a good example of this kind of sale. To compete for the contracts, the oil majors had to "sell" the expertise and technologies that they could bring to bear on a massive infrastructure-building effort, which includes over a dozen of the largest liquefied natural gas (LNG) plants (or trains) in existence. They had to demonstrate that they could muster the billions of dollars in financing needed to build these mega-trains as well as a fleet of newly designed, high-capacity LNG supertankers. They had to convince the Qataris that they could bring the gas to market by winning long-term supply contracts in the United States, Europe, and Asia. Not least of all, they also had to demonstrate their ability to help develop Qatar itself by raising the education level and work skills of the country's citizens, and providing them with jobs. Of course, the rewards are equally large: ExxonMobil won many of the major North

Field contracts, and, as a result, is now positioned to become the world's largest non–state-owned producer of natural gas, a much greener source of energy than oil and one for which demand will likely explode in coming decades.[5]

On the other end of the complex sale scale are relatively simple transactions, often in the thousands or tens of thousands of dollars. Many of the products and services in these sales are considered commodities, but they aren't commodities because the companies that created them have refused to treat them as such, just as I suggested earlier. They include chemicals, industrial gases, electronic components, hardware, and so on.

A good example is the wire clamps used in aircraft to channel electrical wires throughout the airframe. These clamps are sold by the barrel to aerospace manufacturers, airlines, and governments. Aviation clamps certainly sound like a commodity, something a purchasing department might order over the Internet, but some clamp manufacturers embed a lot of value in their clamps. They design them to snugly and safely secure multiple wires in a single clamp, reducing the possibility of a spark, which can endanger the lives of passengers. They color code clamps, allowing for the easy identification of wires in unique subassemblies, and they create easy-release clamps that make it more efficient to secure and access wires in hard-to-reach places.

Aviation clamps don't have to be sold as a commodity. They protect human lives and expensive assets, they speed up the aircraft assembly, and they provide valuable savings in the troubleshooting and repair of planes, reducing the time it takes to get grounded aircraft back into the air. Clamps like this are worth a great deal more than expected and they can be sold at a premium . . . if a clamp manufacturer can design a clamp that offers added value, and the sales force can connect and quantify that value in terms of the customer's performance metrics.

The most common type of complex sale occupies the middle ground between industry-shaking deals and so-called commodities. These sales include information technology, medical devices and equipment, industrial equipment of all kinds, consulting and services—the list goes on and on. They typically range from the tens of thousands to tens of millions.

One example of such a sale is the enterprise-level software used by hospitals and other large health-care providers. These health-care information systems (HISs) streamline, automate, and manage the flow of clinical and financial information. They reach into every department from admissions and billing to nursing to specialized medical functions, such as radiology and cardiology. Typically, one salesperson leads a team of specialists (coding, data collection, functions, solution implementation, and service, etc.) to determine the information requirements within the hospital, and to design a software solution that fully addresses them. The team works with people throughout the hospital. The sales cycle is months, or sometimes several years. The value of the transaction can range from several hundred thousand dollars to several million dollars or more.

The two driving forces of Era 3—complexity and commoditization—are creating a tremendous squeeze in the middle ground of complex sales. For me, the level of the pressure in this size sale was vividly illustrated one day when I sat down with the senior leadership team of an industrial equipment company. This company makes and sells automated circuit-board assembly equipment. These highly specialized machines are capable of placing components of various sizes and shapes onto extremely small circuit boards, like the one in your mobile phone. They shoot all of these various-sized components into cramped spaces at a rate of 60,000 components per hour. They utilize laser positioning and video inspection, and well, it is complex. The company's biggest problem, according to its leaders: these highly engineered $2-million machines had become commoditized. Of course, I'm thinking that if something this complex is being commoditized, we are all at risk!

The one constant that unifies all of the sales I've just described is the customer's need for assistance in understanding all of the ways in which the value offered by the solutions being considered is connected to his or her organization's unique situation and its future performance. In other words, a complex sale is one in which the customer is not fully equipped to make a set of high-quality decisions around the nature of the problem, what to buy to solve it, and how to implement it to realize the solution's value. In fact, if you can provide this assistance to your customers, the process by which you sell and the way in which you sell will become critical components of the value of your solutions and a key source of competitive advantage for you and your company.

There are two additional common characteristics of complex sales that we must recognize. The first is that they require multiple decisions at multiple levels in the customer's organization. In the complex sale, there is no single buying decision. It is a process consisting of a long chain of interrelated decisions, impacting multiple departments and multiple disciplines that will ripple throughout the customer's organization.

The second common characteristic of the complex sale flows logically from the first: Because there are multiple decisions, there are invariably multiple decision makers and decision influencers. Shelves of books are devoted to helping salespeople find, engage, and close the decision maker. In the complex sale, however, the search for this mythical decision maker is fruitless. There is no single decision maker. Certainly, there is always a person who can say yes when everyone else says no, and conversely, there is always someone who can say no when everyone else says yes. Today, however, the best decisions, certainly all high-quality decisions, are the result of orchestrating a consensus.

As we proceed through this book, I will show you how top-performing professionals provide a high-quality decision process (based on scalable principles), create a hypothesis for value, and engage and guide the proper "cast of characters" to a set of decisions that likely weren't fully envisioned at the start of the process. In doing so, they enable their customers to connect the value dots, quantify the value impact, and make a high-return purchase. In essence, they create the decision.

Eliminate the *Dry Run*

Now that we have a good picture of what the Era 3 world and the complex sale look like, let's turn back to the *Dry Run*. In every variation of that scenario, sales professionals are doing everything they have been taught, they are offering high-quality, cost-effective solutions, and yet their conversion rate of proposals to sales is in free fall. Why is this happening?

The answer is that the nature of the complex sale and the opposing environmental forces of commoditization and complexity are making it extraordinarily difficult, not just for sales professionals to bring in revenue, but for customers to fully understand the problems and opportunities they face. The complex sale and the forces that affect it are impairing our customers' ability to make rational purchasing decisions.

Ultimately, that is why salespeople are experiencing so many *Dry Runs*. Their customers were unable to make a high-quality decision. They either didn't understand how the solution being presented would solve their problem, or they didn't believe that the magnitude of their problem was large enough to require action. I am not suggesting that customers are incompetent, although many frustrated salespeople who don't understand the dynamics behind their customers' decisions make exactly that accusation. In fact, our customers are fully capable of understanding complex transactions. The real problem is they don't have a process that can help them to make sense of their situation and then connect it to the right solution. That is the underlying thesis of this book and the key insight that will help you orchestrate and win the complex sale.

The often-ignored reality of Era 3's complex sales environment is that customers need our help. They need help understanding how to analyze the problems they face. They need help designing optimal solutions to the problems they uncover. And they need help implementing those solutions and measuring the value the solutions have created. The next logical question is: what can we, as sales professionals, do about it? The obvious answer is to provide the help our customers require. Unfortunately, because the environment continues to evolve in complexity, most leaders of sales organizations have difficulty figuring out how to help not only their customers, but their own teams.

By and large, sales leaders are more focused on what their competitors are doing and their own sales numbers. The problem with the former focus is that if you look and sound like your competitors, it is more difficult to differentiate your offerings in the customer's mind and you are in danger of self-commoditization. The problem with the latter focus is that too many sales leaders believe that selling is a numbers game. When the numbers don't measure up or it seems like the competition is gaining on them, their typical response can be summarized in two words: sell harder! They try to solve the problem by putting pressure on the system. They command their troops to make more cold calls, set more appointments, give more presentations, overcome more objections, and thus, close more sales. In other words, do more of what's not working.

There are two problems with this approach. First, the number of potential sales is never infinite. At some point, you run out of viable opportunities, and you are forced to start chasing more and more marginal prospects. Meanwhile, the cost of sales goes through the roof. Second, "selling harder" is doing more of the same thing and expecting a different result. That isn't going to happen in complex sales . . . not ever. In the next chapter, I'll show you why that is so.

But before we move on, I'd like to suggest that you sit down with the best minds in your company and think through how you are currently engaging customers. Begin by asking your team these questions: "Are we following our customer's lead, or are we providing our customers with the process and expertise they need to make quality decisions regarding their situation and our offerings? Are we providing an effective level of professional guidance?" To help organize your thoughts, consider that your customers will likely need assistance in one or more of three major areas.

1. First, they may require outside expertise to help diagnose their situations. They may not have the ability to define the problem they are experiencing or the opportunity they are missing. In many cases, they may not even recognize that there is a problem. If they don't know these things, then surely they do not know what it is costing them to continue on their current path. So consider: to what degree do you and your team assist the customer in bringing more clarity to the diagnosis?

2. Second, your customers may not be able to design the optimal solution. They may not know what options

exist, how the solution will be integrated into their current systems, how to measure value impact, and other such considerations. So to what extent do you and your team enable customers to design comprehensive solutions?

3. Finally, your customers may not have the ability to implement the solutions and deliver the expected results to their organizations. So to what degree do you and your team provide the support needed for the customer to navigate the changes required to achieve the maximum impact of your solution?

Your answers to these questions should provide a quick portrait of how well your company and sales force are prepared to master the complex sale.

Avoiding the Traps of Self-Commoditization

Challenge Your Assumptions and Set Yourself Apart

One of the greatest frustrations that senior leaders and their sales and marketing organizations face today is that their customers are treating their high-value solutions as commodities. What they don't realize is that they themselves are probably more to blame for this problem than any external force. Self-commoditization is the biggest threat to success in the complex sales world, and your sales processes and behaviors are likely the largest contributing factor in that exposure.

Think about it this way: Your customers have little or no experience buying the kinds of solutions you sell, and you (and your competitors) are presenting them with reams of solution data that they must sort through, comprehend, and connect to their unique situation on their own. It is as if salespeople were major league pitchers hurling 90-mile-per-hour fastballs at batters, who are either at the plate for the very first time or only step up to the plate occasionally. This is an ideal situation for a major league pitcher—he wants to strike out the batter. But you want the customer to connect. When customers don't understand the value that your products and services can deliver to their companies, they don't buy, and you lose.

If your proposal conversion rate is low and you're experiencing a high percentage of no-decisions, chances are you are striking out far too many customers. You are very likely using a sales approach that is based on a set of assumptions that are not only irrelevant in the Era 3 selling environment, but are actually counterproductive traps that sabotage your sales efforts.

Assumption #1: The Decision Trap

Era 2 selling depends on the customer's decision process. Sales professionals are tasked with determining that process. They are expected to uncover what customers are looking for, what's important to them, what they need, and what criteria they will use to decide the purchase. With this information in hand, the salespeople are directed to create a match by aligning their solutions with each customer's needs and buying process. All of their training is based on the implicit assumption that the customer has a high-quality buying process. This is the decision trap.

I regularly ask the sales professionals in my "Mastering the Complex Sale" seminars to raise their hands if this accurately describes what they have been taught and encouraged to do. Invariably, the room is full of hands held high. Then, I ask the participants to keep their hands up if they think that their customers have a high-quality decision process in place to recognize and understand the problems they solve and the unique value of their solutions. Seldom is a single hand left in the air. As the salespeople look around the room, a disconcerting realization is reflected in their faces: If our customers have flawed decision processes, why are we trying to understand and fit into them?

The problems resulting from deficiencies in a customer's decision process are further compounded by the tendency of Era 2 selling approaches to overlook the distinction between the customer's decision process and the customer's purchase approval process. Customers always bring a "one-size-fits-all" approval process to the sales engagement, but they seldom bring a quality decision process. The failure to recognize the differences and to treat both processes as one and the same also leads to many *Dry Runs*.

Reality Check
Is There a Quality Decision Process?

- Do your customers have a well-defined, high-quality decision-making process in place that enables them to comprehend the value of your unique offering, pre-sale and post-sale?
- Can you separate your customer's decision process from his or her approval process?

You can get an accurate sense of the state of customer-driven decision making anytime and anywhere salespeople talk business together. Think about how many times you have heard or perhaps said yourself: "My customers just don't get it." The reality behind that statement of frustration is not too difficult to figure out. Customers don't "get it" for one of two reasons: you are either overestimating the value your solutions bring to the customer or overestimating the customer's ability to comprehend that value on their own.

Assuming that the solution offered actually has value for customers, the flawed logic behind the "customer doesn't get it" complaint is that the salespeople who say it are, in essence, blaming customers for being unprepared to buy the solutions they are offering. They are implying that customers should somehow be ready to effectively analyze and evaluate complex products and services, such as capital equipment, that they may buy once a year or once every seven years or perhaps just once in their entire careers. Even more illogically, many of these salespeople are assuming that their customers have a high-quality decision process capable of evaluating leading-edge solutions that are appearing in the marketplace for the first time.

The technological leaders in all industries are especially vulnerable in the latter scenario. Their greatest challenge is what Geoffrey Moore calls "crossing the chasm" between the small group of visionary customers who immediately see the value of a new solution or who just want the latest and greatest offerings, and customers in the mainstream marketplace who, through no fault of their own, truly don't yet understand the significance of the new solution.[1]

There is a way to cross the chasm. It requires reducing the uncertainty inherent in the challenges and risks that your customers face. Uncertainty creates indecision, but clarity defeats uncertainty. High-quality decision, change management, and value measurement processes provide the clarity that leads to decisive and predictable customer action. The problem is that conventional sales approaches do not include them.

Assumption #2: The Comprehension Trap

To win the complex sale, your customers must be able to comprehend the problems you solve, the risks they face, your competitors' weaknesses, the unique value of your solution, and much, much more. However, most salespeople are operating on the mistaken assumption that customers have a much higher level of comprehension than they actually do.

The best salespeople walk into an opportunity at much higher levels of experience than their customers. They understand the products and services they are bringing to market because they deal with them every day. In addition, because they spend most of their time with customers, they understand their customers' industries, encounter a full range of operational practices, and often become experts in their customers' businesses. When we at Prime Resource Group shadow experienced, successful sales professionals, we often see them quickly size up a customer's situation. The advanced perspective and comprehension of the experienced salesperson stands in vivid contrast to that of the typical customer. Unfortunately, however, even the best salespeople often assume that their customers know what they know and see what they see. This naturally leads salespeople to believe that their customers are well prepared to analyze their own problems and connect them to the value of the forthcoming solutions.

Reality Check
What Is the Customer's Level of Comprehension?

- To what degree do your customers understand their own problems and the performance risks they face?

- To what degree do they understand your solutions and the financial contributions they will make?

- What is your customers' average level of comprehension of the risks they face and the solution required to mitigate that risk?

I use a tool called the "Decision Challenge graph" to illustrate this basic and often overlooked reality (see Figure 2.1). The graph's horizontal axis represents the customer's position in the decision process. The decision progression ranges from zero, the point at which customers have no idea that there is a problem and see no need to act, to midpoint, where they recognize a problem and are actively considering action, to 100 percent, the point at which customers have made the purchase. The graph's vertical

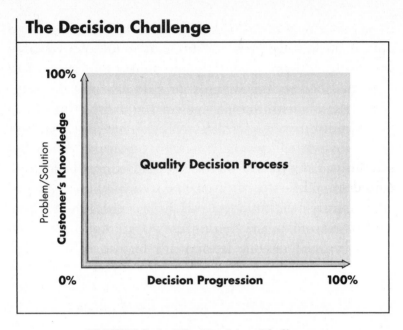

FIGURE 2.1 The Decision Challenge

axis represents the level of knowledge that customers have about their problems and the possible solutions. At zero, customers have no knowledge of the types of problems they may have or the solutions that are available, including the solution you offer. At the top of the scale, they have complete, or perfect, knowledge of their problems and the solutions required to solve them—they know everything needed to make a well-informed, high-quality decision— they know what to look at and for, what to measure, what to compare, what to test, and so on. The field of the graph formed by these two axes represents the customer's overall comprehension.

So here's the big question: If you consider a prospective customer who is calling you for information, where would you place the person or group on each of these axes?

When I ask this question in seminars, here's the response I receive: The average customer has already begun to act. He has entered the market because he knows there is a problem at some level and there are solutions available that likely address it. For the sake of discussion, let's place this customer at around 60 percent on the decision progress axis. The average customer's knowledge of his or her company's problems and the possible solutions to them are less complete. On average, customers have some understanding of the nature of their problem, may have done considerable Internet research, and spoken to colleagues to learn more about the possible solutions, but they don't have a significant depth of knowledge in either area. Let's place this average customer at the 40 percent mark on the knowledge axis. When I plot these points on the graph, this customer's area of comprehension fills just 24 percent of the field (see Figure 2.2). Clearly, he is not prepared to make a high-quality decision.

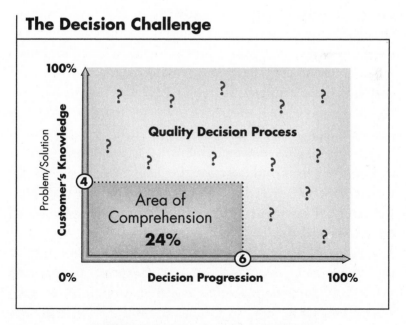

FIGURE 2.2 The Decision Challenge

In other words, the ability of your customers to connect your solutions to their businesses is very limited. They recognize that they may have a problem, but they don't have a clear understanding of what that problem entails, the risk they face, or how the solutions in the market can resolve it. A customer who does not comprehend a solution will probably not buy it, will certainly not buy it quickly, and won't be willing to pay a premium price for it.

Assumption #3: The Presentation Trap

The negative consequences of the first two assumptions are exacerbated by a third assumption: presentation is the best way to educate customers and communicate in a sales process.

Sales organizations devote a tremendous amount of time, effort, and resources to the preparation and creation of compelling presentations. Everything salespeople do in the early stages of the sales process—the prospecting, contacting, and qualifying of potential customers—is aimed at creating an opportunity to present their solutions . . . and the sooner, the better. Everything they do after the presentation—including the preparation of proposals, overcoming objections, negotiating, and closing—is designed to support and reiterate the presentation. The irony is that most of this effort is lost on customers. As the decision and comprehension traps suggest, most presentations are a waste of time.

I'm not saying that presentations do not have a place in a viable sales process. They are, however, plagued by three fundamental problems: content, timing, and audience. Salespeople tend to present too much, too soon, and to the wrong people.

Salespeople hate to hear this: Their companies have provided them with the tools and skills to prepare presentations as the key weapon in their sales arsenal. It is their security blanket, their comfort zone, and they fear giving it up. "Wait a minute," they protest, "our presentations are aimed at educating customers. They will not buy what they don't understand."

That is exactly right, customers will not buy what they don't understand. Even though a presentation can lift the customer's level of comprehension, it is one of the least effective methods for accomplishing that goal. There are three reasons why:

1. A presentation, no matter how glitzy and sophisticated, is just a lecture. The salesperson is the teacher and the customer is the student. The salesperson teaches by telling. The big problem with teaching by telling is that we don't remember even half of what we are told. People retain only about 30 percent of what they hear. The use of visual aids (e.g., a PowerPoint slide show) boosts retention rates to 40 percent, but the generally accepted rule of thumb among learning experts is that more than half of even the most sophisticated presentation will be lost.[2]

2. The vast majority—80 to 90 percent—of the typical sales presentation is devoted to describing the salesperson's company, its solutions, and the rosy future being sold. Rarely do I see a presentation that devotes more than 10 to 20 percent of its focus to the customer and the customer's current situation or problem. Therefore, while a presentation may raise the customer's comprehension level, that gain is mainly centered on the solutions being presented. As we've already seen, however, customers are very often not aware of the existence or exact nature of their problems and the

cost of those problems. As a result, while customers may be greatly impressed with the offering being presented, they still lack a clear understanding of two critical connections: how the offering applies to their situation and the value the offering will deliver to their business. They do not know why they should buy, what risks they face if they do, and thus, lack a compelling reason to change and move ahead with the sale.

Reality Check
Is Your Proposal Off Balance?

- What percentage of your sales presentation/proposal is devoted to describing your company, your solution, and the customer's future?
- What percentage of your sales presentation/proposal is devoted to clarifying your customer's business situation, problems, risks, and objectives?

3. There is a third reason that presentations are a waste of time in complex sales: Your competitors are likely following the same strategy. They are also busy presenting. Unless you have no competition, your customers will be communicating with them. They have meetings arranged with you and one, two, or even more of your competitors. In each meeting, a sales team is presenting the best side of its solutions. Your team is telling the customers that they need the solutions that only your company offers, and your competitors are making the same arguments about their solutions. In every case, the presentations are heavily skewed toward the seller and the solutions and the customer is often left out of the equation.

Look at this from the customer's perspective. Based on what we learned so far, it is highly likely that two-thirds or more of the information that customers hear fall outside their area of comprehension and they don't remember over half of what they hear and see. Further, what they do hear during multiple presentations sounds very much the same. It focuses almost exclusively on the solutions and is not connected to the reality of their unique situations. Leaving the customer to make these connections on their own is a perfect recipe for self-commoditization.

How do customers then respond to competing presentations when they all sound so amazingly similar? Often, they attempt to make the complex understandable by weighing those elements that vendors' offerings have in common and eliminating those elements that do not fit neatly into an over-simplified comparison chart. When this happens, the salesperson's ability to differentiate his or her company's offerings from the competition is subverted, and price, the one common denominator of all offers, again raises its ugly head and is likely to become the deciding factor in the sale.

Customers may also respond by not responding. They listen politely as you "educate" them, thank you for your time, and promise to get back in touch when they are ready to make a decision. This is the setup for the *Dry Run*.

Finally, some customers may actively respond. They may ask you to justify the information that you have presented or challenge the viability of your solution. This is the response that every conventional salesperson is conditioned to expect and trained to counter. The customer objects and the sales professional goes to work overcoming those objections. This sets the stage for the final and most lethal assumption of the Era 2 sales process.

Reality Check
Are You Really That Different?

- In the eyes of the customer, how different is the structure, format, and content of your sales presentation from your major competitors' sales presentations?

Assumption #4: The Adversarial Trap

The final assumption of Era 2 sales processes is the idea that any reluctance on the part of the customer is a direct threat to the sale and the salesperson's success, and thus, these customer "objections" must be overcome. When salespeople start overcoming objections, they are placing themselves in conflict with their customers when they should be establishing collaborative relationships instead. At best, this sets the stage for polite disagreements and respectful differences of opinion, forcing salespeople to defend their solutions. At worst, it turns the sales process into a battle in which the salesperson goes into attack mode in a misguided effort to conquer the customer and win the sale. This might seem like an exaggerated notion to you, but consider the language that appears so often in sales training and in the conversations between salespeople and their managers. Words like "persist," "provoke," "persuade," and "convince" all imply aggressive behavior.

Any hint of conflict between salespeople and their customers is exacerbated by the frustration that results from the miscommunication engendered by Era 2 sales processes. Salespeople are presenting professionally packaged data complete with executive summaries that their prospective customers find either unintelligible or unconnected to their situation. Confused, and with no sound basis on which to evaluate the information, customers respond negatively. Era 2 salespeople, who are overestimating their customers' level of comprehension and decision processes, interpret this as an objection to be overcome and swing into action. "No," the salesperson says, "you don't understand. This is why you need our solution . . ." Now the salesperson is arguing with the customer.

What happens next? If the customer doesn't shut down the presentation altogether, he may offer a second negative response. Another round of verbal sparring ensues. The customer's frustration turns into exasperation. At this point, the sale is in doubt and the salesperson knows that the customer needs the solution, so he escalates his efforts to convince to buy. The downward spiral accelerates.

This downward spiral often occurs in the most polite and respectful terms. But, no matter how civilized the exchange, the net result is that the salesperson and the customer have become adversaries. The sale has turned into a battle . . . a battle in which the customer always has the final say.

Reality Check
Are You Challenging or Collaborating?

- Do you find yourself debating with customers?
- Are your customers reacting defensively and/or challenging your recommendations?
- How much of your time with customers is spent presenting, persuading, and convincing?

There are unfortunate exceptions, but, for the most part, salespeople using an Era 2 approach aren't purposely trying to beat up their customers. They are simply following the accepted dictates of a sales process that generates flawed statements that drive self-sabotaging sales behaviors such as:

> "Whether they know it or not, every qualified prospect needs your products and services."
>
> "The ability to persuade is the key ingredient of successful selling."
>
> "If you are persistent and pursue the customer at regular intervals and with increasing intensity, you will eventually get a sale."
>
> "An objection is a signal to convince the customer to buy."
>
> "Real selling doesn't start until the customer says no."

There may be a kernel of truth in each of these statements, but they also represent many of the sales techniques that customers find irritating. They turn selling into a competitive game in which someone, either the salesperson or the customer, must lose. In reality, both lose when collaboration could have created mutual value.

I'm not saying that the adversarial mind-set won't produce sales. It will. It's "sales, James-Bond style." Every sales organization has a James or Jamie Bond on the payroll, and too many managers are looking to hire more of them. You can drop the Bond-style salesperson out of an airplane into any territory, with any prospect, any product, any quota, and you know he or she will come back with the business.

The problem with the Bond approach is that there is always a lot of collateral damage. People are going to get hurt on both sides of the table. Many salespeople, and even managers, try to rationalize this away and depend on their service and support functions to repair the damage. But the service person's saying, "I'm sorry, you know how salespeople can be," may not cut it. Customer relationships are fragile, memory is long, and customers have options.

In the real world of business, where margins are tight and a few percentage points of additional cost turn a profitable order into a loss, the Bond style can also quickly become a major liability in terms of total cost of sales. Coerce customers to do something they aren't sure about or promise what you can't deliver, and sales engagements will quickly become less profitable. Further, with today's instant communications, negative perceptions spread very quickly, which can make new business acquisitions even more difficult and expensive.

Systematic Self-Sabotage

These aren't the only erroneous assumptions in the conventional selling process. There are others, blatant and subtle, that harbor traps that negatively impact key performance metrics, including margins, proposal conversion ratios, sales cycle time, and forecasting accuracy. I will discuss more of these in later chapters, but for now, all you need to recognize is that conventional selling processes have inherent flaws that cause the companies and their sales forces that use them, to unintentionally but systematically sabotage their own efforts.

The first trap of conventional selling causes salespeople to depend on their customers' decision-making processes, which are almost always insufficient. The second, closely related trap is sprung when salespeople also assume that customers are able to understand their own problems and evaluate solutions at a level that enables them to discern the true value of the salesperson's unique solutions.

Because they assume higher levels of comprehension and decision-making ability on the part of their customers than actually exist, salespeople focus the majority of their efforts on presentations. In falling into the presentation trap, they largely ignore the customers' world, the most significant source of credibility, differentiation, and decision criteria in any sale—thus creating a major disconnect between customers and solutions. Competing at the solutions level and rushing to present information heightens the blur between competitive solutions. This reinforces customers' drive toward commoditization by validating their view that all the solutions are the same.

Even worse, the emphasis on sales presentations exacerbates the communication gap between buyer and seller, leading to frustration, misunderstandings, conflict, and adversarial relationships—all of which impede the salesperson's ability to create the cooperative and trust-based relationships with customers that are needed to win complex sales. This is a major cause of the protective behaviors customers so often adopt when dealing with salespeople.

These problems are what the famous quality guru and statistician W. Edwards Deming defined as systemic problems. They are inherent to Era 2 sales processes and they can't be solved by managerial harangues about working harder, motivational talks, or imposing more hours of training in presenting, handling objections, and closing. The only effective and enduring way to solve these problems is to set aside Era 2 sales processes. What is needed in their place is the topic of the next chapter.

A Proven Approach to Winning Complex Sales

You're Either Part of Your System or Somebody Else's

_____

Systems, Skills, and Disciplines

A theory that explains how to sell successfully in Era 3, or explains anything else for that matter, is a product of abstract reasoning. It is someone's speculation about the nature of an activity or process, and it may, or, as is too often the case, may not be, an accurate reflection of the physical world. What validates a theory and makes it worth adopting and emulating is that it works in everyday practice in real conditions. That's why for the past 28 years, my colleagues at Prime Resource Group and I have often begun our consulting engagements by shadowing the most successful sales professionals in the companies with which we work.

Our goal has been to decode and replicate the practices of these high-performing sales professionals. They typically represent the top 3 to 7 percent of the sales organization and are selling at a rate that is three to five times the average. We want to understand what they believe, how they think, and how they interact with their customers and colleagues. We've studied their reasoning and behavior patterns, and the thinking and methods behind their success.

Shadowing top-performing salespeople quickly led us to an interesting observation: Generally, they don't rely on conventional selling techniques and they rarely follow their company's standard sales processes. They are not using their company's sales brochures and other collateral, reciting prepared pitches and presenting, or manipulating customers in an overt effort to close sales. I'll describe what they are doing later in the chapter, but for now let's just say that top performers are not selling . . . at least, not in the conventional sense of the word.

In fact, the success of top performers is often a mystery to their employers and their colleagues. They are considered anomalies—rare exceptions to the rule whose success is a natural, but irreproducible, phenomenon. This is compounded by the fact that many top performers can't clearly articulate the reasons behind their own success. When we ask them to explain themselves, we often find ourselves in conversations like this:

> *"Was there a particular reason you didn't bring out the product brochures on this appointment?"*
>
> *"I don't know," the salesperson replies. "They seem to distract the customer."*
>
> *"In what way?"*
>
> *"Well, if I hand out the brochure, the customer usually starts asking a lot of product questions."*
>
> *"Is that a bad thing?"*
>
> *"I guess not," the salesperson says, "but I know when I spend all my time talking about our products, I usually don't get the sale. So, I rarely, if ever, use the brochures."*

These top performers are not being cagey. Rather, they have developed a personal approach to selling and communication through a long period of trial-and-error experimentation. Once they've achieved success, they tend to suppress all the pain they went through to perfect their process. Also, they are too busy winning sales to spend time documenting what they are doing and analyzing how and why it works. This is why they are seldom able to explain in a clear fashion why they do what they do, and when asked they say things like, "It just seems to work" or "It felt like that was the right thing to say." Not very instructive. Nevertheless, their hard-won knowledge is an extraordinarily valuable foundation for a model of sales excellence.

Over the years, we've worked very hard to translate "seems to work" and "felt like" into tangible and teachable principles and practices. We've studied how they connect to research and theories in organizational and behavioral psychology, decision science, emotional intelligence, interpersonal dynamics, and change management. We have also examined how other professions, such as medicine, aviation, law, and engineering, developed the competencies required to replicate with consistency the "best practices" of their top performers. This combination of theory and practice has enabled us to develop and refine a platform for complex sales in Era 3 that companies can adopt and adapt into an organizational capability, and a sustainable competitive advantage in the marketplace.

This platform, which we've named Diagnostic Business Development, is organized into the same three primary elements that define all professions: systems, skills, and disciplines.

1. A *system* is a set of procedures and an organized process that leads to a repeatable, consistent, and therefore, predictable result. The system represents the "what to do" to succeed in Era 3's complex sales environment.

2. *Skills* encompass the sales professional's knowledge and ability to utilize the tools and techniques needed to succeed in the complex sale. They represent the "how-to" of successful Era 3 selling and enable salespeople to execute the system.

3. *Discipline* is the mind-set of the sales professional; it is his or her attitude, standards of performance, and mental and emotional stamina. Discipline is the inner

strength and courage that supports the "will do" of the successful Era 3 salesperson.

I've organized the insights we have gained over the years into these elements for a good reason: A successful professional must be proficient in all three. All professionals, including pilots, accountants, engineers, doctors, and lawyers, among many others, are called on to learn, practice, and master each of these elements. Pilots, for instance, must follow many systems to operate their aircraft. They use tools, such as navigational aids, and master skills to execute those systems. Finally, they must embrace a discipline or a mind-set that enables them to remain cool, calm, and collected while performing their jobs, whether that entails cruising on autopilot at 55,000 feet or executing an emergency landing on the Hudson River. To be able to speak of selling as a profession, we need to define and refine a body of knowledge—the systems, skills, and disciplines that enable sales professionals to achieve their fullest potential and the best results.

A Value-Driven, Diagnosis-Based System for Complex Sales

Value is a critical concept in the Era 3 complex sale. No salesperson can afford to ignore value because it is the only thing that our customers are willing to pay for. Accordingly, an Era 3 sales system must enable sales professionals to connect and quantify value for their customers and to measure and verify that their customers actually achieved the value promised.

Please note that the word "communicate" did not appear in the last sentence. Most salespeople are unable to manage the value challenge because they are being taught and equipped to "communicate value messages" to their customers. In other words, Era 1 and Era 2 sellers are trying to force fit the concept of value into their existing sales approaches. As a result, the flaws in their approaches bleed through. They end up presenting a superficial version of value and do not connect it to the customer in a credible, tangible way. When salespeople communicate value in this way, it ends up being another barrier to a successful sale. What we want to do to master the complex sale is clarify value. Value clarity is achieved by connecting specific aspects of your value to the relevant customer performance metrics that your value impacts, and quantifying such impact in a number that your customer believes.

The two driving forces of Era 3, complexity and commoditization, make the efforts of salespeople to communicate value even more ineffective. Commoditization encourages customers to ignore value in the quest for the lowest price. At the same time, the increasing complexity of our solutions and the problems they are designed to address make value comprehension ever more difficult for customers. For all of these reasons, value has been more of a buzzword than a tangible reality in complex sales.

The Diagnostic Business Development system (or the Prime Process, for short) makes customer value a tangible reality because each of its four stages is designed to connect and quantify value in a lock-step progression. Thus, as you lead your customers through the process, their value comprehension grows in a consistent and measureable manner.

Further, the Prime Process offers sales organizations a platform on which to understand and integrate their professional skills and develop and apply a mental discipline. This represents a quantum leap beyond sales training, which is usually skill-based and leaves salespeople with a briefcase full of tools but no systematic way to apply them to achieve their ultimate goal.

It is a meta-process, one that can be scaled and over-laid on any sale, and is particularly relevant to the complex sale. It provides a navigable path from the first step of iden-tifying potential customers, through the sale itself, and on to expanding and retaining profitable customer relation-ships. Thus, it is a system that encompasses all of the criti-cal activities of the sales professional and provides the decision-making guidance that customers involved in a complex business decision so desperately need.

Finally, as I'll discuss in Part 3, the Prime Process can also become the basis for an organizational capability that can be extended and applied to produce customer value from product inception to customer consumption. In doing so, it can enhance the communication and cooperation be-tween major business functions, from R&D to marketing to sales to service and support.

Because the Prime Process covers all elements of the complex sale, it naturally encompasses a great deal of infor-mation. To facilitate comprehension and ease of use, I've divided the process into four subsystems or phases. The phases of the process are related in a linear fashion and are organized by the major activity that is undertaken in each specific phase. They are Discover, Diagnose, Design, and Deliver (see Figure 3.1).

Discover

The Discover phase of the Prime Process is where a sales-person translates the broad, market-segment–based value propositions of his or her solutions into a value hypothe-sis that is custom designed for an individual customer. When you do this properly, not only does your customer decide that it is worthwhile to investigate the validity of the hypothesis, he also decides he should investigate it with you.

Diagnostic Business Development

Stage	Agenda	Value Life Cycle	
		Value Proposition	Capability
Discover	• Prepare • Engage	Value Hypothesis	Premise
Diagnose	• Identify • Quantify	Value Required	Incentive to Change
Design	• Create • Align	Value Expected	Confidence to Invest
Deliver	• Implement • Measure	Value Achieved	Document Results

FIGURE 3.1 Diagnostic Business Development

Discover is about the research and preparation. It encompasses how sales professionals get ready to constructively engage and serve customers. Every sale starts at the same point—the identification of a potential customer. In Era 1 and Era 2 selling, this was called prospecting and qualification, two tasks that were, unfortunately, often characterized by minimal preparation. In Era 1, it included anyone who could fog a mirror. In Era 2, it was anyone who belonged to a generic market segment. In the Discover phase, however, we expand preparation into a process that is aimed at the identification of a specific customer who has the highest probability of change.

Discover requires pushing beyond the traditional boundaries of prospecting to create a solid foundation on which to build a long-term, profitable relationship. It recognizes the fact that every qualified prospect will not become a customer. It embraces that realization by actively looking for reasons to disqualify a prospect and refusing to unnecessarily waste the time and resources of the prospect or the sales professional.

The tasks in the Discover process include pre-contact research of potential customers and their industry. Discover also includes the preparation of an engagement strategy, which includes an introduction, basic assumptions about the value that could be created (the value hypothesis), and a conversational bridge designed specifically for a single individual within a customer company. In addition, it includes the initial conversation with the prospective customer, during which the value hypothesis is discussed and the customer and sales professional mutually decide whether the Prime Process should continue.

In the Discover phase, as in each succeeding phase of the Prime Process, salespeople are actively building a perception of themselves in the customer's mind. In this case, that perception is one of professionalism. We want customers to understand that mutual respect and trust—governs our relationship. We want them to see us as competent, as well versed in their business, and as a contributor or source of competitive advantage.

Diagnose

In the Diagnose phase of the Prime Process, the validity of the value hypothesis is tested and, if it is found to be an accurate reflection of the customer's reality, the value required is identified and quantified. This phase provides the customer with the incentive to change.

The Diagnose stage encompasses how sales professionals help their prospects and customers fully comprehend the risks they face and the opportunities that are missing. It is a process of hyper-qualification during which we use carefully constructed and sequenced diagnostic questions to conduct an in-depth determination of the extent and financial impact of the customer's situation.

Most Era 2 selling methodologies recognize the importance of understanding customers' problems and, accordingly, often include some form of needs analysis in their process. However, the true intention of needs analysis is usually subverted. First, we find that it is used to get customers to describe what they need. In essence, they are asked to diagnose themselves even when they don't clearly understand their problems, as in, "What are your issues?" Second, the questions that salespeople ask their customers are more often about the customers' buying process than their situation, as in "What are you looking for? Who will make the decision? When will you make the decision? Do you have a budget in mind?" These questions are aimed at advancing the sale rather than establishing the customer's actual situation. Finally, and in the worst cases, needs analysis is used as a highly biased and nonvalidated generic critique designed to justify the salesperson's solutions. This is another example of the bleed-through that occurs when useful techniques are applied in a flawed approach.

In the Prime Process, diagnosis is not subordinate to the solutions being offered or the sale. It is meant to maximize objective awareness of the risks that customers face and their dissatisfaction with their current situations, whether that dissatisfaction supports the salesperson's offerings or not.

It is during the Diagnose phase that the Prime Process most radically diverges from the selling approaches of earlier eras. In the more traditional approaches, salespeople are looking for the decision to buy after the presentation and during the close. Our research tells us that the customer makes the two most critical decisions—to buy and from whom—during the Diagnose phase, much earlier in the process than most salespeople realize. If you grab hold of this one fact, it will enable you to drastically reduce the amount of time you devote to *Dry Runs*.

During the Diagnose phase, we uncover the physical evidence that will support or refute the value hypothesis offered in the Discover phase and quantify the actual cost of the customer's problems. At this point, we need to deepen our understanding of our customers' businesses and their job responsibilities, perspectives, and concerns. Diagnosis also includes a collaborative effort to evolve a comprehensive view of the problem with our customers, thus allowing them to make an informed decision as to whether they need to change.

In the Diagnose phase, we want our customers to see us as credible. We establish our credibility by our ability to identify, evaluate, and communicate the sources and intensity of their problems, as well as helping them recognize opportunities that they are not aware of. We reinforce that credibility by refusing to alter the customer's reality to fit our own needs.

Design

The Design phase of the Prime Process defines the value expected, that is, how would a solution address the customer's situation and what would be the financial impact of the resultant value. This phase of the process provides the customer with the confidence to invest.

Design encompasses how salespeople help the customer create and understand the solution. It is a collaborative and highly interactive effort to help customers sort through their expectations and alternatives in order to arrive at an optimal solution.

In conventional sales approaches, design equals presentation. In presentation, however, the customer is not involved in the design of the solution; it is something that the salesperson cooks up back in the seller's office. As a result, customers do not develop a significant degree of ownership in the solutions being offered to them. The Era 2 salesperson said, "This is the product we offer that is best suited to your situation." Then he will proceed to list a litany of features and technical information specific to that solution.

In contrast, the Design phase of the Prime Process is not focused on a specific solution. Instead, its goal is to get sales professionals and their customers working together to identify the optimal solution to the problems that were uncovered and quantified in the Diagnose phase.

There is an important distinction here. An optimal solution does not mean the product or service that we are charged with selling right now is best suited to the customer's problem. Rather, the optimal solution is a series of product or service parameters that minimizes the customer's risk of change and optimizes return on investment. By staying true to the objective of a quality business decision, where that solution will be found is a secondary consideration at this stage in the decision process.

The tasks included in the Design phase are aimed at establishing and understanding the decision criteria the customer will use to find a solution to the problem. This goal requires us to establish the solution results the customer would expect, the quantifiable business values for those outcomes (and thus, determine the appropriate funding for the acquisition of the solution), and the timing in which it must be delivered. We manage customer expectations during the Design phase by introducing and exploring alternatives, including solutions offered by competitors. We also teach customers the questions that they should be asking of all potential suppliers to ensure a quality decision.

In the Design phase, we want our customers to see a high degree of integrity in all our behaviors. We establish our integrity by creating a solution framework that best solves their problems. It frames a set of decision criteria that we would use to determine what to select for ourselves or would recommend without hesitating if our best friends were experiencing this particular problem. The conclusion of the Design phase provides the final version of what we call a discussion document. This document provides a summary of the diagnosis with a "pencil sketch" of the solution. It is used to do a final sanity check with your customer before you create a formal proposal. It is the dress rehearsal, your final run-through, and it ensures that there will be no surprises during the final stage of the Prime Process.

Deliver

The Deliver phase confirms the acceptance of the proposal and then verifies and measures the value achieved after the customer has implemented your solution. This phase of the process proves that you are a full-fledged business partner and compels the customer to maintain an ongoing relationship with you and your company.

In the Deliver phase, the work of the previous phases comes to fruition. Deliver encompasses how the salesperson ensures that the customer has succeeded in obtaining the value promised by the solution and can measure and verify the financial impact of the solution.

While conventional sales processes force salespeople to overcome objections and try to close the sale at this point in the process, none of the pressures of closing exist in the Deliver phase. This is because the Prime Process allows customers to formulate their own decisions through a logical, evolutionary process. Customers who have traveled through the Prime Process have a clear understanding of their challenges, and they know what the best solution will look like. In fact, they have become co-authors of that solution. That is why sales professionals who use the Prime Process, and have not disqualified the customer by its final phase, experience exceptional conversion ratios. That is also why the final step and ultimate goal in the Deliver phase is not to close the sale, but to maximize the customer's awareness of the value derived from the solution that is being implemented.

The tasks in the Deliver phase begin with the preparation and discussion of a formal proposal and the customer's official acceptance of the solution. The next steps include the delivery and support of the solution and the measurement and evaluation of the value that has been delivered. The final task of the Deliver phase is to serve the customer and grow the relationship.

In the Deliver phase, we want our customers to see us as dependable. We literally do what we said we were going to do and deliver on the value we promised. As we complete the sale, our customers should be thinking: You are here for me and you will take care of me. I can depend on you now and in the future.

*   *   *

The four phases of the Diagnostic Business Development system—the Prime Process—represent a fundamental re-engineering of the conventional sales process. The process eliminates the inherent flaws in the sales processes of previous eras, directly addresses the gaps in our customers' decision processes, and helps ensure that sales organizations connect the value of their companies' solutions to their customers' situations. It is a process done *with* the customer in a very transparent fashion, not a process done *to* the customer in a covert manner.

The Right Set of Skills for Complex Sales

The second element of any profession encompasses the knowledge and skills that its practitioners need to achieve their goals and the tools that support the skills. In Diagnostic Business Development, most of the skills and tools are applied in specific phases of the Prime Process, and I will discuss them in later chapters. But there are three major skills and their associated tools that span the entire selling process.

These skills and tools help successful sales professionals answer a critical set of questions that are present in every Era 3 complex sale:

- How is value created within your customer's business?
- Who should be involved in determining the existence and financial impact of the problem?
- What are the problems the customer is actually experiencing or the risks to which he or she is exposed?
- How are those problems impeding the customer's ability to accomplish his or her business objectives?
- How are the problems affecting your customer's customer?
- How will the customer achieve successful business outcomes?
- How are those outcomes connected to the salesperson's solutions?
- Who should be involved in the design and the implementation of the solution?

The answers to these questions can be stated in the form of an equation that must be solved to successfully navigate a complex sale:

Diagnostic Selling

Right People + Right Questions + Right Sequence = Quality Decisions

Right People: Managing the Cast of Characters

In Era 3, salespeople must be skilled at identifying and assembling the network of people who are needed in order to answer the questions mentioned previously and reach a quality buying decision. The single decision maker, as we saw in Chapter 1, is a myth. So too is the idea that the customer, without assistance, can assemble the best group of people to be involved in this work. Logic dictates that if our customers don't have quality decision processes, they won't be able to identify and assemble the right decision teams.

There is another reality that sales professionals must recognize. A customer's decision team is not just a group of people who have the power to say "yea" or "nay" to the sale. A quality decision team must be far more comprehensive, including people who can assist in the diagnosis of their current situation and the identification of the best solution. Thus, the task of assembling the right team of decision makers, advisors, and influencers is now more sophisticated and complex than ever.

One telling observation from the field is that when it comes to identifying and interacting with a network of decision makers, advisors, and influencers in a complex sale, the most successful salespeople don't passively accept the decision team identified by their customers. They take an active role in building the optimal "cast" with their customers. They seek to identify the important cast members in the customer's organization, involve each in the decision process, and ensure that each has all the assistance required to comprehend and quantify the problem, the opportunity, and the solution and its results. Effectively managing the decision team is a job that spans the entire sales process.

A very important characteristic of the cast of characters in a complex sale is perspective. In every sale, there are two major perspectives: The problem perspective includes members of the customer's organization who can help identify, understand, and communicate the details and consequences of the problem. The second perspective, the solution perspective, includes those who can help identify, understand, and communicate the appropriate design, investment, and measurement criteria of the solution.

The challenge of casting the complex sale doesn't stop here. We need decision team members who can bring to the surface the problem and solution perspectives available at different levels within the organization, such as executive and managerial levels, and operational and functional levels. Sometimes, depending on the sale, we may also need to include cast members from outside the customer's company, such as the customer's customers and business partners who might also be affected by a decision.

Why go through all this work? The obvious answer is that there is no other way to ensure that you are developing all of the information required to guide your customer to a high-quality decision. There are also other less obvious reasons. For instance, would you prefer to present a solution to a group that has had little or no input into its content, or would you rather present a solution proposal to a group that has already taken an active role in creating it? Would you prefer to deal with a newly installed decision maker who has replaced your single contact in the middle of the sales process, or would you rather face that new decision maker with the support of all the remaining cast members and with full documentation of the progress already made? The answers to these questions should be clear.

The successful sales professional assembles and orchestrates the group of players who have the most information, insight, and influence on the decision to buy. This shortens the sales cycle by effectively reaching the right people, creating a sense of urgency, and helping them make high-quality decisions. A full cast also helps sales professionals overcome the unexpected surprises that sink sales, enhancing predictability and increasing the chances of a successful engagement.

Right Questions: Quality Conversations, Vital Information

All salespeople are taught to use a variety of questions in the sales process, but most use them in ineffective ways and in dubious pursuits. They ask questions to get their customers to volunteer information that they think is critical to win the sale, such as, "How will you buy?" and "What will you buy?" They ask future-oriented questions that have little connection to the customer's current problems versus present-oriented questions that tap into the evidence of urgent problems and risks. Worst of all, the questions they ask subvert the most valuable use of questions—to diagnose.

The most successful sales professionals are skilled and sophisticated diagnosticians. They understand that to effectively and accurately diagnose a customer's situation, they must be able to create a conversational flow designed to ask the right people the right questions. The diagnostic questions that these salespeople use to understand and communicate customers' problems include:

1. *A to Z* questions, which frame a customer's process and then enable the salesperson to pinpoint specific areas of concern within it.

2. *Indicator* questions, which uncover observable and quantifiable symptoms of problems.

3. *Assumptive* questions, which expand the customer's comprehension of the problem in nonthreatening ways.

4. *Rule of Two* questions, which help identify preferred alternatives or respond to negative issues by giving the customer permission to be honest, without fear of retribution from the salesperson.

These diagnostic questions, which I will detail in the chapters that follow, are purposely designed to avoid turning our conversations with customers into rote interviews, useless fishing expeditions, or worse, irritating interrogations. Instead, they help salespeople develop conversations in which the customer's self-esteem is protected, communication is stimulated, and mutual value is generated. (Silence and listening skills, as I will describe later, also play important ancillary roles in diagnostic questioning.)

Most importantly, they enable sales professionals to ask questions that customers have not thought to ask themselves. These questions expand the thinking of customers and their comprehension of their situations. Therefore, they stimulate the decision to change and create exceptional credibility for the salesperson in customers' eyes.

Right Sequence: The *Bridge to Change* and Value Clarity

Just as complex sales involve multiple decision makers, they also require multiple decisions. The content and sequencing of those decisions is what allows us to connect our customers and the problems they face (or the value they require) to the value inherent in solutions we are offering. In short, this creates value clarity. To accomplish this goal, we need to establish an ordered, repeatable sequence of questions that will guide our customers through a series of high-quality decisions.

The sequencing of questions must be custom designed for your solutions and it must be navigated in different ways according to the physical reality of each individual customer. All sequenced diagnostic maps[TM] are based on a generic format that I call the *Bridge to Change* (see Figure 3.2).

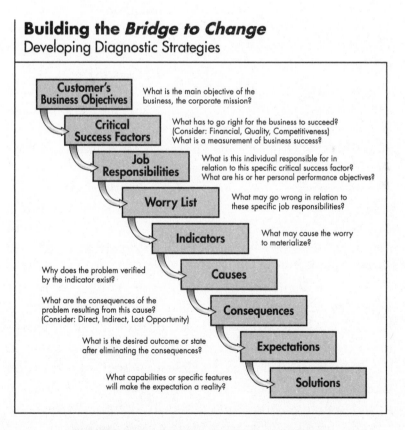

FIGURE 3.2 Building the *Bridge to Change*

The *Bridge to Change* is patterned after the tools and methods that physicians use to diagnose complex medical conditions and prescribe appropriate solutions. It guides salespeople by establishing a question flow, in a decision-tree format, that is capable of leading their customers through complex decisions. More importantly, it allows salespeople to pinpoint the areas in which they can construct value connections that will benefit their customers.

The bridge has nine main links; each increases the customer's value clarity. It starts at the organizational level by examining the customer's major business objectives or drivers and the critical success factors (CSFs) that must be attained to achieve those objectives. It seeks to identify the individuals responsible for each CSF and to understand their job responsibilities and personal performance objectives. The bridge prompts the salesperson to identify value gaps by probing for the physical evidence of performance shortfalls and risk, uncovering their causes, and quantifying their consequences. In its last links, the bridge helps define the expectations and alternatives for solving the customer's problems and then narrows the search to a final solution.

When the *Bridge to Change* is customized for your solutions, it serves as a decision tree that maps value. You and your customer can follow this decision tree to diagnose missing value, create solution parameters, and finally, identify the metrics that indicate value achievement. The value of a decision tree is that only the branches that are relevant must be followed. Thus, it offers a very effective means of quickly homing in on the areas in which your solutions offer the greatest value to the customers. When each relevant branch of a decision tree has been completed to a customer's satisfaction, all of the potential objections have, by definition, been resolved. In fact, when you hear customer objections, what you are actually hearing is a lack of value clarity, the direct result of a skipped or incompletely followed branch. The customer can, of course, still refuse to buy/change, but it is unlikely that his or her refusal will be based on any reason within the salesperson's control.

When we build decision trees for our clients, we reverse engineer the Value Life Cycle. We start with the myriad elements of value that can be delivered by their solutions. Then, step by step, we track each element back to the physical evidence that would be present and observable in our client's customer's business if that value were not present. This is the evidence that proves his or her performance is at risk in absence of the solutions our client provides.

The construction and design of decision trees is a complicated process that becomes more and more difficult and more and more involved as solution complexity rises. For instance, when we created a decision tree for one client, it quickly grew to over 650 branches. But the rewards for undertaking this effort are correspondingly high. The decision tree provided our client's sales team with just seven questions that the team could ask to quickly identify not only whether a prospect was a viable customer, but also which specific branches of the tree would offer the highest value to that customer. Perhaps the most interesting outcome of this effort was that by providing its sales engineers with a standardized, consistent means of mapping customer value, the client was able to reduce the time it took for a graduate sales engineer to become proficient and operate profitably from 5 to 7 years to just 12 to 18 months.

* * *

The cast of characters, diagnostic questions, and the *Bridge to Change* are the key skills of the diagnostic sales professional. They also represent the three components of the complex sales equation: right people, right questions, and right sequence.

The Discipline for Mastering Complex Sales

The final element of the Diagnostic Business Development platform is the discipline with which top-performing salespeople approach their work. In Era 3, this is perhaps the most critical component of their success. Just as the flawed assumptions of Era 2 sales methodologies doom those who accept them to ineffectiveness and miscommunication, the mental framework with which we approach today's complex sale acts as the enabler of all that follows. Without the proper mind-set or point of view, the best systems and skills cannot be consistently executed.

Three statements summarize, in broad terms, the mind-set or discipline needed to succeed in Era 3's complex sales.

1. *The most successful sales professionals recognize that a sale is, first and foremost, the result of the customer making a decision to change.* Thus, when they are working with a customer, they are actually helping the customer navigate through a decision process rather than a sales process. This is a critical distinction in terms of the salesperson's mind-set: A decision process is aimed at assisting the customer in making the best choices. A sales process is aimed at moving goods and services. Further, all the decisions that customers make during a sales engagement add up to one thing: whether or not to change.

All too often, a sales professional uncovers a serious problem within a customer company, which the customer acknowledges and wants to solve. They discuss the solution options together, the customer agrees that the salesperson has a solution that can eliminate the problem, and yet, the customer does not buy. Why does this occur? It occurs because the customer cannot or will not go through the personal or organizational changes required to obtain the value that the solution promises.

Every sale—whether complex or not—is based on a customer's decision to change. In simple sales, the customer's decision and the change process are often transparent, but they still take place. Consider what takes place when I purchase copy paper: I notice that I've just loaded the last ream of paper into the machine. I consider the consequences of not being able to make copies if I run out of paper and decide that I must do something about it now. I think about the easiest way to obtain more paper. I decide to order it from an online superstore that offers low prices and free delivery within 24 hours. The process and decision may occur so quickly that I don't even notice what I've done, but nonetheless, a sale has occurred only because I made several decisions about whether and how to change my situation.

Of course, in simple sales, like buying copy paper, customers understand the risk involved in the change and therefore, their resistance to making the change is low. But what happens as the complexity of the sale increases? The degree of investment, the requirements for successful implementation, and the emotional elements of the sale, such as its impact on the buyer's career and livelihood, create an escalating risk of change. With higher risk comes greater resistance to change. This is why change and risk management play such major roles in complex sales.

The more complex the sale, the more radical the change that the customer must undertake, and the greater the actual and perceived risk becomes. A salesperson, who has a selling mind-set, is solely focused on presenting and selling his or her solutions and is ignoring the critical elements of managing decisions, risk, and change. The most successful salespeople, on the other hand, are noted for

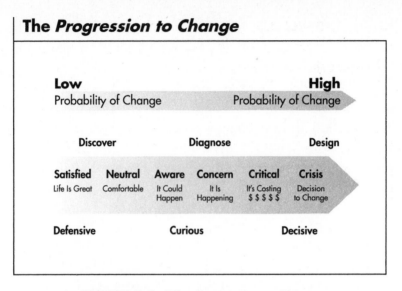

FIGURE 3.3   The *Progression to Change*

their ability to understand and guide the customer's change progression (see Figure 3.3).

A key insight in the large body of psychological and organizational research concerning the dynamics of change is that the decision to change is usually made as a response to negative situations and, thus, is driven by negative emotions. People change when they feel dissatisfied, fearful, or at risk in their current situations, and customers are more likely to buy in those same circumstances. Conversely, customers who are satisfied with their current situation are unlikely to buy.

When salespeople ignore the customer's *Progression to Change* (shown in Table 3.1), sales outcomes are jeopardized. Here is a common scenario: The salesperson focuses on presenting and selling the future value that will accrue from his offering. He does a wonderful job presenting, being positive and enthusiastic and eventually lifting the customer to a euphoric peak with his company's exciting and unique solution. It is the perfect time to close and, of

TABLE 3.1 *Progression to Change*

Progression to Change

Satisfied	"Life is great!" Customers have strong feelings of success. They feel their situation is very good and see no need to change.
Neutral	"I'm comfortable." Customers have no conscious feelings of satisfaction or pain. They are not actively exploring their problems, and they are not considering change.
Aware	"It could happen to me." Customers understand that the issue can be a concern and happens to people in similar positions. They recognize they may be at risk and they recognize that "it could happen to me" or "it happens to people like me or companies like us."
Concerned	"It is happening to me." Customers have some discomfort and notice the indicators or physical evidence of the problem. They recognize that the problem is potentially harmful and they must further clarify the problem.
Critical	"It is costing xxx dollars." Customers have an extremely clear picture of the problem and are able to recognize its financial impact in their environment. They know that they need to make a decision to change or not.
Crisis	"I must change!" Customers recognize that the situation is bad enough relative to other issues they are facing, and a decision to change is made.

course, that is exactly what the salesperson attempts to do. What happens next? The customer, being asked to commit, is shocked out of the positive future and confronted with the current reality, which includes his company's other priorities, budget, and all the risks and issues associated with change. The customer's resistance to change rears its ugly head. Objections are raised, the sales process slows down, and the sale, which the salesperson thought was nearing completion, is in danger of being lost.

The best salespeople, on the other hand, understand that all customers are located somewhere along a change spectrum. As these salespeople approach the sales process from a risk and change perspective, they deal directly, and in real time, with the critical change and risk issues that their customers must resolve. Instead of selling a rosy future, they focus on helping their customers identify the consequences of staying the same or not changing their negative present. When they help customers understand the risks of staying the same and quantify the specific financial costs or lost revenues related to staying the same, the decision to buy (which is the decision to change) takes on a compelling urgency. Customers are not dealing with an optional future but with the immediate reality of a problem that they must solve. Because so few sales professionals approach their sales engagements with this change-oriented mind-set, those few who understand and focus on the customer's decision to change enjoy a distinct advantage and a unique position in the marketplace.

When salespeople work with their customers from the perspective of a decision to change, they avoid the conflicting agendas of buyers and sellers. Typically, there are two agendas at work in a sale: (1) the customer's agenda, which is often represented by a buying process imposed by the purchasing department and is primarily designed to obtain the lowest price; and (2) the seller's agenda, which is often represented by a selling process that is designed to move products and services at the highest price. These two agendas, with their conflicting goals, naturally generate tension and mistrust. Working from the perspective of a decision to change, however, allows the salesperson and the customer to work toward a mutual objective—understanding the customer's problem and business objectives, and aligning the desired outcomes with the best available solution. This places the customer in a position to make the highest-quality decision regarding the proposed change.

2. The second focus of the most successful sales professionals is on the development of the customer's business. That is, successful salespeople think like business owners.

We call this mind-set *business-think*, and sales professionals who adopt it act as business advisors to their customers and thus are regarded as contributors to their customers' businesses.

When I suggest to salespeople that they should serve as business advisors to their customers, they invariably and unanimously agree. They have heard this before. But their thinking process becomes very clear when we ask them what happens after the customer agrees to buy. The typical answers include "we coordinate the installation," "we train the customer," and "we get paid." The interesting thing about these responses is that they are focused on what the salesperson and his or her company do next. The business being developed is the salesperson's, not the customer's.

When we ask the best sales professionals what happens after their customers agree to buy, they say things like, "They are on their way to achieving their objectives," or "We can start to measure the customer's results in terms of reduced costs or increased revenues." The business they are developing is the customer's business.

Approaching a sale with a *business-think* mind-set means that sales professionals develop the acumen and take the time necessary to understand the financial, qualitative, and competitive business drivers at work in their customers' companies. It means that, as business advisors, they frame their communication with customers in terms that customers understand and that matter to them. Finally, it means that when the sale has been consummated, sales professionals measure and evaluate success from their customers' perspectives and make sure that their customers achieve the value promised during the sale.

A discipline of *business-think* also has profound implications for how sales professionals perceive and manage their own careers and the resources of their companies. When you approach your work with a *business-think* mind-set, you quickly realize that your resources are limited and must be focused to achieve their greatest potential. You know that you can't be all things to all customers and will devote your energy only to the best opportunities available. You come to respect your time and expertise, and view yourself as a valuable resource. You also expect your customers to do the same. Successful salespeople do not waste time in situations where their solutions are not required. Instead, they gravitate toward the opportunities where their services are most needed and highly valued.

I describe the behavior that results from this discipline as "going for the no." It is a mind-set that recognizes that at any given time, only a small percentage of customers in a complex sale market will change/buy. Therefore, we must quickly identify those customers who won't buy and set them aside for later attention. The best sales professionals are willing to ask the hard questions, the questions to which the answer could confirm that there will be no sale. Compare this attitude to that of the Era 1 and Era 2 salespeople who are taught to always be going for the yes. They allocate their time equally among the entire universe of opportunities, and when they get in front of potential customers, they stay there as long as possible—often pressing to remain in the engagement even after customers have disqualified them. These salespeople will not only avoid the questions that could end the sale, they will go so far as to consciously ignore the signals that suggest the sale will not happen. These salespeople aren't treating their own time and expertise with respect, and it shouldn't come as much of a surprise when their customers don't either.

3. To succeed in complex sales, the most successful salespeople are building customer relationships based on trust and cooperation. You could argue that all salespeople are working hard to create trusting, cooperative relationships with their customers. However, while that may be true in theory, it has not been translated into reality in the customer's world.

In the mid-1990s, researchers asked almost 3,000 decision makers, "What is the highest degree to which you trust any of the salespeople you bought from in the previous 24 months?" Only 4 percent of those surveyed said that they "completely" trusted the salespeople from whom they had bought. Nine percent said that they "substantially or generally" trusted the salesperson. Another 26 percent said they "somewhat or slightly" trusted the salesperson, and 61 percent said they trusted the salesperson "rarely or not at all."[1] Remember, these are the responses of customers about the salesperson from whom they decided to buy! What did the respondents think of the salespeople from whom they decided not to buy?

As we have already seen, this negative perception of salespeople is a problem caused by the assumptions inherent to Era 1 and Era 2 sales processes. Accordingly, the only sure way to break through the interpersonal barriers between salespeople and customers is to abandon these outdated sales processes.

The most successful salespeople do not exhibit conventional sales behaviors, which, by the way, research has shown decreases trust. For instance, they avoid taking positions of certainty and saying things like, "This will work the best" and "This is what you need."

How do successful sales professionals behave? There are three role models that reflect the behavior of these professionals: the doctor, the best friend, and the detective.

The Doctor

Doctors normally provide a great model that sales professionals can relate to and emulate. Even though the medical profession has its own image problems, let's consider the ideal.

Doctors take an oath to "do no harm;" that is, they do their best to leave patients in better condition than they find them. They accomplish this goal through the process of diagnosis. Picture a middle-aged, overweight male walking into a doctor's office. Does the doctor observe the patient's appearance, note that he is a "qualified" candidate for a bypass, and try to sell him surgery? Of course not; it would be absurd. Doctors recognize that in order to determine what is best for a patient, they cannot prescribe the same cures to broad segments of patients. Instead, they must diagnose each patient individually by studying his or her unique condition and situation.

It is common for salespeople to meet with customers and prescribe solutions despite the fact that many of those customers may not be truly qualified candidates for their products and services. The best sales professionals, however, act like doctors, diagnosing each customer's condition individually, bringing great clarity to the customer's situation, and prescribing solutions that fit the unique circumstances of each case. Accordingly, their customers see them as professionals who are willing to take the time to understand their problems and who can be trusted to offer solutions that not only "do no harm," but also improve the health of their businesses.

The Best Friend

When I say that the best sales professionals act like their customers' best friends, I don't mean that they try to get invited to their customers' family gatherings. Best friends are often as close to us as family members, but they embody other qualities as well. Picture the most trusted person in your life—a spouse, parent, colleague, teacher, coach, or advisor. That is the degree of trust that the best salespeople seek to achieve when they adopt the best friend model.

We expect our best friends to look out for our best interests. They help to protect us from errors in judgment. We also look to our best friends for honest opinions and answers. We trust them to tell us the truth.

The best salespeople use the role of best friend as a litmus test. They are constantly asking themselves, "If this customer were my best friend, what would I advise in this situation? How would I respond to this question? Do I have their best interests in mind or my own?"

The Detective

The third role model that successful sales professionals reference is the detective. I'm not talking about the aggressive, kick-the-door-in Hollywood detective who beats confessions out of suspects. Rather, I'm talking about the kind of detective who delights in applying his or her intellect to solving mysteries.

These detectives are naturally and incessantly curious and they often have a low-key, nonconfrontational style. Think of Tony Shalhoub's portrayal of Adrian Monk and Peter Falk's classic Detective Columbo on television, or the detectives in Agatha Christie's mysteries, Miss Marple and Hercule Poirot.[2]

These detectives don't become emotionally invested in the outcomes of their cases. They don't threaten suspects; they remain cool, calm, and collected. They rarely even raise their voices. They are mild-mannered and non-threatening to the point of appearing ineffective—a characteristic that causes everyone involved in the case to underestimate them and relax. The suspects feel safe and secure, and the detectives quietly go about the business of solving the case.

These detectives solve their cases by observing the minutest details of the situation, by asking a seemingly endless number of polite, unassuming questions, and by reaching objective, rational conclusions that are supported by physical evidence. By the way, these methods provide an excellent contrast to James Bond's methods. The king of collateral damage, Bond already knows all the answers, so he doesn't need to ask any questions. All he needs to do is provoke a fight and win it.

The best sales professionals emulate the mild-mannered detective. They seek to fully understand what is happening in the customer's world, and they achieve this goal in the same way that detectives solve their cases, through the power of observation and the process of questioning and clarifying everything they notice.

* * *

To illustrate how the doctor, best friend, and detective role models come together in the behavior of the most successful sales professionals, consider this example. It is very common for customers to ask quite early in an engagement, "What makes your solution better than competitor A's?" How does the typical salesperson respond to this? That's right, by launching into presentation mode and reciting a long litany of attributes that may or may not be relevant to this particular customer's situation. The sales professional, however, steps back and says, "I'm not sure that it would be in your case. Competitor A is a great company and has some great solutions. At this point, I really don't understand enough about what you are experiencing and trying to accomplish to be comfortable suggesting a solution, whether it's ours, theirs, or someone else's. Let me ask you this . . . "

This response horrifies a large percentage of salespeople. It's nowhere in their repertoire. But if you think about it, this is a doctor refusing to prescribe without diagnosis, a best friend refusing to recommend something that might jeopardize the relationship, and a detective refusing to act without evidence. Why wouldn't you respond in the exact same manner to a prospective customer?

The objective of your behavior should be to build trust and create an open collaboration with customers. Traditional sales moves tend to shut communication down. You'll find that the best sales professionals, for the most part, are literally doing the opposite of what most salespeople do. It's not natural, it's counterintuitive, but it's extremely effective.

Creating Value Clarity with Diagnostic Business Development

The systems, skills, and disciplines encompassed in the Diagnostic Business Development platform enable sales professionals to clarify the value they deliver to customers in three dimensions. In ascending order of complexity, profitable return, and competitive advantage, these dimensions are the Product, Process, and Performance levels of value.

At the Product level, the value focus is on the product or service itself, which is a focus on the seller and his or her solution. Product functionality, quality, availability, and cost are the major sources of value clarification at this level. Typically, the salesperson is dealing at the operations level or with the purchasing department and competing with similar products and services. The major concern at this level is that you can do very little to differentiate a product.

Era 1 sales strategies tend to be limited to creating value at the product level. They make only the most tenuous value connections with the customer. Thus, in their customers' eyes, this is a commodity sale and subject to the price pressures described in Chapter 1.

At the Process level, the delivery of value is expanded from the product (or service) being sold to the process in which the customer will use it. Here the focus is on the customer and his or her business processes. The optimization of the process becomes the major source of value clarification at this level. Typically, the salesperson and his or her team are working with operating managers in the various departments at a tactical level. Your solution often becomes an integral part of a process improvement effort.

At the Process level of value, sales professionals are creating a sort of limited partnership with the customer. In their customers' eyes, this sale delivers a greater degree of value than a product-based transaction, but the relationship has shallow roots. It can easily lose its value for the customer once the process is optimized or if the process becomes outmoded and the customer eliminates or outsources it. The Era 2 sales approach tends to focus on value at the Process level.

The Performance level offers the greatest potential for value clarity and it is the highest value level which a sales professional can achieve. The focus is on the strategy and performance of the customer's business. Achieving the customer's strategic objectives becomes the major source of value at this level. Typically, the sales professional is working with senior executives, as well as the operations level. The sales professional and customer recognize that the solution has value ramifications across multiple business processes and boundaries. The sale is only one manifestation

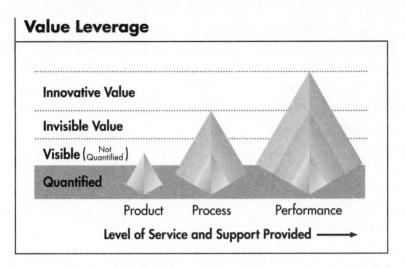

Value Leverage

Innovative Value

Invisible Value

Visible ($_{\text{Quantified}}^{\text{Not}}$)

Quantified

Product   Process   Performance

Level of Service and Support Provided ⟶

FIGURE 3.4 Value Leverage

of an ongoing relationship that is connected to the customer's organization at an enterprise level.

In Era 3, the best sales professionals are connecting and quantifying value at the Product and Process levels, but their ultimate objective is to reach the Performance level. At this level, they create strategic partnerships with their customers. In their customers' eyes, the sale is an investment in a more profitable future and the relationship with the seller is a valuable asset and source of competitive advantage. Relationships like this are not easily uprooted (see Figure 3.4).

In terms of value clarity, it is important to note that I'm defining customers in a broad sense that includes all of your company's go-to-market channels. For instance, if you are delivering products and services through a distribution network or wholesaler partners, you should be considering how to clarify value at the Product, Process, and Performance level in order to enhance each business entity. Value can be created at every level within your distribution network in each business, up to and including your customer's customer.

To recap, we now have discussed the systems, skills, and disciplines that comprise the Diagnostic Business Development platform. In the next four chapters, I will describe each phase of the Prime Process in greater detail to show you how the systems, skills, and disciplines work together in the quest to master the complex sale.

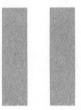

The Four Phases of Diagnostic Business Development

Discover the Prime Customer

Entering at the Level of Power and Influence

Discover is a critical phase in the complex sale because it is when we create the foundation upon which the initial opportunity and the long-term relationship with a customer are built. Unfortunately, salespeople often overlook and underestimate the power of a solid foundation. The greater our ability to customize and personalize the engagement strategy and approach for individual customers, the more likely it is they will see that we are speaking directly to their situations and their individual job responsibilities. This enhances the probability that we will be invited into their organizations and they will see our offerings as relevant and having a substantial impact.

The goal of the Discover phase of the Prime Process is to identify those customers who are most likely experiencing the issues our solutions address and are missing the value we could provide; therefore, they have the highest probability of buying our products and services. In this initial phase, we establish a profile of the ideal customer that is derived from the value capabilities of our offerings, how value is created within our customers' businesses, and the potential constraints in their ability to achieve the value of our offerings. We then identify a specific customer who fits this profile and craft a customized engagement strategy based on a *value hypothesis* that is relevant to that customer. A value hypothesis is the first step in the Value Life Cycle. It is about the customer and the potential risks to which his or her company may be exposed. It invites the customer to explore that risk as part of a collaborative effort. Finally, we discuss the value hypothesis with the customer and, if warranted, agree to test its validity by moving into Diagnose, the next stage of the Prime Process. The Discover phase encompasses all of the preparation activity before the formal diagnosis. Think of it as the discovery process that an attorney undertakes before going to court.

In their zeal to get face-to-face with customers, too many salespeople put far too little time and effort into preparation. An alarmingly high percentage of salespeople continue to "wing it" as they approach high-level executives. In fact, the typical attitude toward preparation usually runs along these lines: If the customer walks like a duck and quacks like a duck, a good salesperson should be able to sell him anything made for ducks or, for that matter, anything made for birds. The problem is that this one-size-fits-all attitude toward customers just doesn't fly, nor should it. It is unprofessional, disrespectful, and certainly ineffective.

Customers shut down when they are approached in this way with good cause. First, they know that in the salesperson's eyes they are simply another target among many. They justifiably suspect that any salesperson who sees them as one more target among many is highly likely to subject them to a long-winded, one-sided presentation, high-pressure closing tactics, and other transparent and annoying sales manipulations. Further, because their unique characteristics, job responsibilities, and situations have been largely ignored by salespeople who behaved like this in the past, customers have little basis for believing that whatever this salesperson will offer will create any value for them at all. Thus, they believe that any time they spend with the salesperson will be wasted and they feel completely justified in resisting any level of engagement.

The fact that customers actively resist generic approaches is only one of the reasons that salespeople should avoid them. It is also logically flawed. The commonly accepted idea is that to maximize their success, salespeople should maximize the number of prospects they see and the number of proposals they present. If you extend this logic,

Key Thought™
If You Commoditize Your Customers,
They Will Commoditize You.

When you target customers based on generic qualifications that may or may not actually characterize their companies and situations, you are guilty of treating them exactly the same way that so many salespeople complain that they and their solutions are treated—like commodities. To avoid this trap, you must create an engagement strategy that customers believe could not have been crafted for any other person but themselves.

it suggests that you should spend less time preparing to engage customers in order to see more prospects and give more presentations. Of course, it doesn't work that way. Spending time with prospects when you aren't prepared to engage and who are unlikely to buy is both inefficient and ineffective.

If you want to maximize sales results, you cannot simply engage as many prospective customers as possible and allocate your time equally among them. *Instead, you must concentrate on customers who have the highest probability of being negatively impacted by the absence of your solution and, therefore, will have a correspondingly high probability of being receptive to your solution.* The identification of these potential customers, and the preparation required to create compelling and ultimately successful engagements with them, is the purpose of the Discover phase. If you rush through this phase, you end up gambling your time and resources on vague and unsubstantiated opportunities and, subsequently, your sales results will be less robust, random, and unpredictable.

Key Thought
Is There Someplace Better I Could Be?

Top performers keep the profile of the optimal customer front of mind by continually asking themselves a simple but fundamentally radical question: *Is there someplace better I could be?*

They understand that the best place to be is where they can leverage the value of their solutions to maximize the performance of their customer's business, which will, in turn, maximize their sales results. They are always navigating toward that optimal engagement. They accomplish this by continually gauging the evidence that supports a quality decision and recognizing that when that evidence decreases to the point where the odds of success become more attractive if they engage a new customer, that is exactly what they should do.

How can you identify your best opportunities? Through a more comprehensive and creative approach to the Discover process—an approach that enables you to achieve the following goals:

- Develop a clear understanding of the market for your company's unique and differentiating value.
- Design the most effective strategy, including a value hypothesis that is both highly relevant and material, for the executive in the customer company with whom you will engage.
- Conduct the initial conversations in a way that quickly establishes value relevancy, encouraging the executive to invite you in and provide access to the right people and substantive information.

- Establish a diagnostic agreement that sets the stage for the next phase of the Prime Process.

A good way to manage goals of the Discover phase is to divide it into two stages: In the first stage, sales professionals prepare for the initial engagement by building the value hypothesis, and in the second, they enter the engagement and execute their strategy. Let's take a closer look at these goals, how they are achieved, and how they add up to successfully complete the Discover phase.

Understanding Your Distinctive Value

Before salespeople attempt to understand their customers' worlds, they must develop a full understanding of their own environment and capabilities. More specifically, they need to understand their offerings and the value they can deliver, their potential markets, and the quantitative and qualitative levels of activity they must attain to reach their personal performance goals. This is the proper basis for a guiding vision that sets the best sales professionals on the path to defining the ideal customer.

The vision begins with the *value proposition* inherent in the goods and services that you are offering customers. In the context of complex sales, when I talk about value propositions, I mean the positive business and personal impacts that your offerings are capable of creating for your customers. This value represents your competitive advantage in the marketplace. It also forms a baseline from which you can begin to measure the connection between your offerings and the impact it can have on your prospective customers' business performance.

The unique characteristics of your offerings help you define the ideal customer. If you are selling a logistics software package that allows a company to manage and co-ordinate tens of thousands of small packages with different destinations, the best place to spend your time is not with a company whose shipping patterns indicate that it trans-ports full containers to only a limited number of destina-tions. Obviously, this customer will not be able to achieve the full value offered by your solution.

The analysis of the value proposition yields valuable conclusions about the characteristics of the most qualified customers for your solutions. For instance, if your company is a leader in innovative solutions, you should be looking to engage customers who exhibit the characteristics of early adopters in your target markets. If you are the high-value supplier in your industry, you should be looking for cus-tomers who are positioning themselves as high-value sup-pliers in their respective markets. Value propositions tell us what segment of the industry is most likely to buy, what size company we should contact, and who we should seek out inside those companies. This information allows us to begin constructing an external and internal profile of what our ideal customer looks like.

This is common sense, but it is surprising how often I have seen companies change their value propositions with-out integrating those changes into the way the sales force operates, how often changes in the selling environment render an existing value proposition ineffective, and/or how often salespeople simply don't understand the value proposition they are offering.

Think of the value proposition as the description of the type of value that you can bring to a specific segment of customers. That segment will have similar external and internal profile characteristics. (A value proposition, how-ever, is only a starting point. Eventually, it needs to be translated into a value hypothesis; that is, a statement that is crafted specifically for an individual customer, which must be tested before it can be accepted as valid.)

Pinpointing the Prime Opportunity

Once we understand what an ideal customer should look like, the focus of the Discover phase hones in on an individual company. The most successful salespeople first make sure there is a match between their ideal customer company and the external profile of the company that they intend to contact. Then, they must begin to investigate the internal profile of the company to ensure that it also matches. They are looking for *early warning indicators*, that is, preliminary signs that there is a connection between the customer's business situation and the value that they can deliver. In order to establish the existence of early warning indicators, they identify the business objectives and critical success factors within the customer, and the initial physical evidence that would suggest its performance is at risk. As you may recall, this is the first step in the *Bridge to Change* that I introduced in Chapter 3.

By completing this work, sales professionals create a basis for an initial engagement that is *relevant*, meaning that it is aligned to the customer, and *personal*, meaning that it couldn't have been made with any other individual contact. It will enable them to speak with individual contacts within the company in the company's language, frame initial conversations around issues of importance, and build a perception of professionalism in the customers' minds. It clearly differentiates the sales professional from his or her competition.

An external customer portrait tells us what customers look like from the outside. It includes their demographics, information such as the company size and revenues, industry and market position, and key characteristics that differentiate it from its competitors. An internal profile has two dimensions: how and what the individuals within the customer company think—I call this *psychographic* evidence—and what they are actually experiencing—what I call *physical* evidence.

Psychographic evidence includes information about how a company's leaders and employees approach and perceive their world—the organization's strategies and business culture, its driving forces and goals, and the attitudes and beliefs that underpin the behavior and decision making of management. The physical evidence includes clues to the tangible and relevant conditions within the company that will likely drive a decision to change and, accordingly, determine the outcome of the sale itself.

> **Key Thought**
> **When Working with Limited Resources in a Highly Competitive Environment, Establishing Relevancy Is Crucial.**
>
> In a complex sale, we are dealing with organizations where access is constantly sought and is tightly controlled. It is difficult to reach into the cast of characters, and when we do engage, there is precious little time to differentiate and establish our value. Developing a full understanding of the customer before we make formal contact maximizes our chances of establishing the relevancy required to achieve a constructive engagement and develop the level of access required to accomplish our goals.

There are myriad resources that a salesperson can tap into to gather both psychographic and physical evidence before they formally engage the customer, and research becomes easier every day because digital technologies have placed so much information at our fingertips. There are customers' annual reports, web sites, industry publications, existing suppliers of noncompetitive products, industry contacts, professional and social networks, employees in the customer company . . . the list goes on and on.

Today there is no excuse for engaging with a customer using a generic approach. Just as an example of the depth of information accessible on very short notice, we recently received an inquiry from a global software company regarding our consulting services. That same day, I visited an online business networking site and searched for the company name. I found four individuals linked to my contacts. We were able to contact all of them—including a former vice president of sales and an executive in the company's Asia Pacific region. One of our managing directors was then able to return the call and discuss the client's situation with a considerable degree of understanding and ask some very relevant questions.

The quality of our research has just as much to do with the content and analysis of the data we collect as its sources. One effective way to analyze an organization is in terms of its business drivers, which are usually expressed as critical success factors, strategic goals, or business objectives (see Figure 4.1). It is important to be able to align the value of your solution to your customer's business drivers. This is not difficult if you think of the drivers in terms of three major categories:

1. *Financial drivers* are indicated by goals specifying either top-line growth via increased revenues or bottom-line growth via reduced expenses.
2. *Quality drivers* are indicated by goals based on increasing the satisfaction of the organization's customers, employees, or, for those in heavily regulated industries, regulators.
3. *Competitive drivers* are indicated by goals related to creating innovative new products and services and

Understanding the Business Drivers

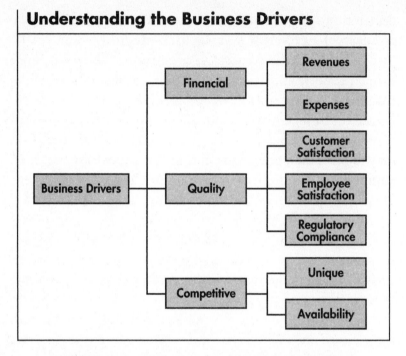

FIGURE 4.1   Understanding the Business Drivers

ensuring the availability of products and services to customers.

To identify long-term drivers, go to the customer's web site and read the corporate mission and vision statements. For short-term drivers, read the CEO's message in the most recent annual report. It is a rare message that does not include concrete statements about the critical success factors driving the business currently and what will drive it in the near future.[1] Next, confirm that the drivers identified in these sources are current (they can change fast) and ask yourself: To what degree are they at work in my prospective customer's business? How do they connect to my offerings?

Then, work at understanding the corporate culture in a customer's company. Personality and values trickle down from the top, so the smart profiler pays particular attention to the customer's senior executives and board members. What are their backgrounds? Their past work experience—in terms of the functions and the previous companies in which they may have worked—can offer important insights into the perspectives of CEOs and other leaders. For instance, a CEO with a sales background may be focused on customer satisfaction, one with an engineering background may be focused more on innovation, and one with a finance background will likely be focused on ROI.

The recent history of an organization also yields valuable clues to the atmosphere and personalities that you can expect to encounter when you contact customers. Has the company restructured recently? Have there been workforce reductions, mergers, or acquisitions? All of these events leave a mark on the organization and offer clues as to what objectives and emotions are driving their decision-making criteria.

There really are no limits to the possibilities for creative customer profiling in the Discover phase. Here is an example that I witnessed in working with a major player in the trucking industry as it launched a comprehensive logistics management service. The company's ideal customer profile called for a manufacturer who was a business process innovator, and the sales team set its sights on earning the business of a major computer manufacturer. One way in which the sales team developed its understanding of the potential customer was by spending several days positioned outside the company's manufacturing facilities. The team counted the number of trucks inbound and outbound, and totaled the number of trucking companies represented. Team members spoke with drivers at local truck stops to get a sense of the size of the loads, their origins, and final destinations. They then used the raw data they collected to create a picture of the computer maker's logistics flow and to calculate estimates of related costs. When the sales team met with the computer manufacturer's managers, they were astounded by the sales team's depth of knowledge about their operation and intrigued by a value hypothesis that estimated the significant value that could be achieved using the new logistics service. They elected to pursue the matter further and eventually transferred all of their logistics business to our client.

Key Thought
Exceptional Credibility

Expected credibility is what you know about your solution and your business. Exceptional credibility is what you know about your customer and his or her business.

I'm not suggesting that you should start camping out at your customers' facilities. The point I'd like to make is that the better your profile of a potential customer is developed, before you initiate contact, the greater your ability will be to create a strong value hypothesis. You will be able to craft a one-of-a-kind introduction—one that your customers will feel was prepared specifically for them and could not be used with anyone else. This is the kind of preparation that enables the best sales professionals to quickly hone in on the customer's critical issues, establish themselves as professionals, and differentiate themselves from the competition. In short, it creates a compelling platform for a constructive engagement and immediate and complete access to the customer.

Diagnostic Positioning—Creating a Compelling Engagement Strategy

When the external and internal profiles we develop confirm our view of a prospective customer as a Prime customer, it is time to create an engagement strategy for the initial customer contact. There are two elements in an engagement strategy. The first element is unchanging and comprises the mind-set with which we should always approach our encounters with customers. The second element has two components: the identification of the best entry point into the customer's organization and the creation of a value hypothesis, a unique and testable statement of the potential risks to which a specific customer may be exposed without your value.

Breaking Type

There are several ways that successful salespeople play against type in their initial contact with customers. I've already introduced the first in Chapter 3—*going for the no*—which is the idea that as sales professionals we should always and actively be looking for reasons to end engagements with individuals whom we can't help. When we are willing to break off or suspend an engagement with a customer who is not experiencing a problem that our offering can solve, we play against the stereotypical salesperson who never takes no for an answer.

An extension of the concept of *going for the no*, and another way in which the most successful sales professionals play against type, is to *always be leaving*. How do most salespeople appear to customers, relative to "staying" or "leaving?" They look like furniture—they're not likely to leave. Those who are most persistent may even seem like a pesky little pitbull clamped on the customer's ankle. The more the customer tries to shake it off, the tighter those little jaws clamp down. To be rid of the stereotypical salesperson, customers expect to have to hang up the phone mid-sentence or call in security. Salespeople who are unwilling to end engagements leave their customers feeling pressured and annoyed.

However, when sale professionals indicate their willingness to step back or even leave the customer engagement, customers feel free to communicate openly and without fear that the information they share will be used against them or cause the salesperson to clamp onto their ankles. You can and should communicate these always-be-leaving attitudes from the very beginning of your contact with customers.

Key Thought
In the Eyes of Customers, Salespeople Are Guilty until Proven Innocent.

This may sound harsh, but it is nonetheless a reality that sales professionals must be prepared to face. The most effective way to break through a customer's preconceived notions about salespeople is to do something actors call "playing against type." When we act in unfamiliar ways, customers are jarred into seeing beyond the stereotypical character they have come to expect.

One last way the best sales professionals play against type is by *being prepared to not be prepared*. The stereotypical salesperson feels pressured to always have an answer. Part of the reason lies in human nature itself; no one likes to admit not knowing the answer to a question. Another part is that a conventional salesperson sees a customer's question as a golden opportunity to start presenting, so he or she is always ready to answer any question and immediately spin it into a discussion about his or her solutions. If you listen to politicians being interviewed, you can often see this kind of spinning in action—you can also see how irritating it is to be on the receiving end of their rhetoric.

Again, however, the best sales professionals break type. Because they are completely prepared, they can afford to be relaxed, engaged, and ready to listen. They don't need to force an answer or spin a question to pitch their products and services. They feel very comfortable in refusing to answer before they fully understand the customer's situation. Even more important, they understand that when they do have an answer, if the customer is not prepared to hear it or won't fully understand its implications, it might very well not be the right time to offer it.

How do these three behavioral concepts manifest themselves in a sales conversation? Think about how you might respond if, very early in a sales engagement, a customer asked you, "What makes your product better than your competitor's product?" The natural response is to launch into a dissertation about the unique benefits of your offering, but when you do, you are fulfilling the image of the conventional salesperson. The counterintuitive—and much more productive—response is to step back from the challenge and say, "I'm not sure that it would be better for your situation. Our competitor makes a fine product, and at this point, I don't understand enough about your situation to recommend which product may be a better fit for your application. Let me ask you this . . ." Then go on to ask a diagnostic question. Sales professionals who respond in this manner are *going for the no* by admitting that it is possible that their solution may not be better. They are demonstrating their willingness to leave by not jumping into presentation mode. Finally, by having a calm and relaxed response at hand, they are clearly prepared to not be prepared. In doing these things, they put the customer at ease and open the door to a more in-depth discussion and greater involvement.

The key goal of this counterintuitive approach to engagements is to create *diagnostic positioning*. In other words, you are positioning yourself to move into the Diagnose phase of the Prime Process. This is very different from the positioning that conventional salespeople are pushing to establish in their initial contacts. They are positioning for their presentations—whether or not the customer will derive value from their solutions and whether or not the customer can fully comprehend and connect that value to his or her company's situation. By now, it should be obvious why this is so often a setup for *Dry Runs*.

Identifying the Optimum Point of Entry

The first component of the second element of engagement strategy is the identification of the best point of entry into the customer's organization in order to collect the information you will need to create the value hypothesis. For most salespeople, the point of entry is usually determined by the job title of the individual who frequently buys their products. Sellers of manufacturing equipment call on production engineers and plant managers; sellers of software call on information technology managers, and so on. All are in search of the sole decision maker, that mythical character who, as I have described, does not exist in complex sales.

The problem with this fixation on job titles is twofold:

First, every conventional salesperson in your industry is calling on the same person inside the customer's organization, so that individual has had significant practice at putting up barriers and restricting access. Even if you can successfully run this obstacle course and make contact, your ability to differentiate yourself from every other salesperson who has gone before you is severely limited. Because of the frequency with which the "usual suspects" must deal with conventional salespeople, they are typically immune to even the best moves.

Second, the usual suspects are often not the best initial contact. It isn't unusual to find a major disconnect between the individuals who are experiencing the impact of a problem—I call them the victims—and those who are tasked with buying the solution. In fact, we almost always find that the managers that salespeople target for their initial contact are those who historically purchased similar solutions, as opposed to those who are experiencing the consequences of the problem and the impact of the absence of the value. These are frequently not the same people.

Key Thought
Who Gets the Call in the Middle of the Night?

The best sales professionals seek to enter the organization through the door of the victim—the person who is experiencing the symptoms of the problem to the degree that would most likely drive a decision to change. Often, this is the person who "gets the call in the middle of the night" when things go wrong—that is, the person who experiences the consequences of the absence of your value. When you track those consequences up the chain of command to the executive level, you will often find the ultimate victim.

Successful sales professionals, on the other hand, are entering customer organizations through less obvious and more productive avenues of access. They identify the best entry points by locating the individuals whose ability to accomplish personal and professional goals is being restricted by a problem and the lack of a solution. Very often, it is these victims who start the chain reaction that leads to a corporate decision to buy. You can be the catalyst for that reaction by identifying and engaging victims throughout the organization, especially the senior executive whose performance is most threatened.

For instance, when we worked with the company that sells the manufacturing systems that place components on printed circuit boards (mentioned in Chapter 1), we found that its salespeople, as well as its competitors' salespeople, were contacting manufacturing and production engineers. That's who typically purchases these machines and runs the manufacturing lines in which they are used. However, as we worked with this client to develop an optimal entry strategy, we discovered that these engineers are not always the victims of the absence of value. In fact, the manufacturing and engineering departments were much less concerned with being able to insert smaller size components than they were with keeping everything running smoothly and on budget. After all, they didn't have any orders for boards with those components. The reason they didn't have any orders was because their sales teams—the real victims—were being forced to pass up bids that called for the installation of these smaller components.

This suggested an entirely new point of entry. We designed a Discover process in which the sales team at our client's company called salespeople at prospective customer companies and simply asked, "Have you lost any sales because your company can't place these components on circuit boards?" If a salesperson said yes, the sales team asked a few more questions to determine the dollar amount of the lost business and extrapolated it across the customer's sales team. This provided the basis for a compelling value hypothesis.

In one of the first calls that the equipment maker's sales force made using this new approach, one salesperson made a few calls to salespeople at a prospective customer and discovered that they had in fact turned away $8 million worth of new business because the current production equipment could not place the components in question. He prepared a value hypothesis for the vice president of sales—the ultimate victim—at the customer company. The VP brought our client's salesperson to the vice president of operations, who in turn called in the head of manufacturing engineering—the traditional buyer of the equipment—and told him to seriously consider acquiring the new equipment.

The victim concept is a very powerful tool that often turns up unexpected insights. After the first edition of this book was published, we worked with a company that sells software that reduces downtime in process manufacturing plants. Its salespeople were calling on plant managers, the highest-ranking managers in a plant, but they were experiencing far too many *Dry Runs*. When I asked one of the company's salespeople to describe one of these *Dry Runs*, he told me how he had very professionally discovered that a certain refinery had an average of two unplanned shutdowns per year at an average cost of $2 million per incident. Then, he described how he established that a $300,000 investment in his company's software could eliminate those costs, netting the refinery's owners $3.7 million annually. He told me how the plant manager nodded in full agreement every step of the way, but when the salesperson tried to close the sale, the manager refused to sign the deal.

"What went wrong?" asked the mystified salesperson. There were only two possibilities: Either the plant manager didn't believe he had a problem or he didn't believe the software would work. As we re-examined the sale, we eliminated the latter alternative—clearly the plant manager believed the software worked. Then we looked closer at the problem. When we called the plant manager, we discovered that, unbeknownst to the salesperson, although the refinery did lose money because of unplanned shutdowns, the downtime had been built into the plant manager's operating budget and performance targets. In other words, if the refinery went down twice a year at a cost of $4 million, the manager didn't have a problem. The plant manager had what I call *normalized pain*—it existed, but it didn't hurt him. However, if the plant manager spent $300,000 on the software, he had a budget overage that represented a very real threat to his performance. Plus, he would be exposed to all the usual implementation risks. Thus, no sale.

"Who does have a problem because the plant manager didn't buy the software?" I asked the salesperson. "Who is the victim in this decision?" The salesperson thought a moment and said that the refinery, along with four other refineries in the region, were all the responsibility of a regional vice president. His eyes lit up as he realized that if this vice president spent $1.5 million on software for all five refineries, he could add $18.5 million worth of production to his region's targets annually. Further, the vice president had P&L responsibility, so adding that lost revenue back into the region's bottom line would be a coup. The salesperson contacted the vice president and within 90 days had a signed deal to install the software in all five plants.

Creating the Value Hypothesis

The second component of the pre-contact preparation stage of an engagement strategy is the creation of the *value hypothesis*. Far too many salespeople use what I call a "value assault" approach for their initial customer engagements. The value assault is all about the solution, its positive value, and how it will greatly improve the customer's business. It

> ## Key Thought
> ## The Victim Is Much More Receptive and Communicative Than the Perpetrator.
>
> The individuals in a business whose performance measurements are adversely affected by a business problem or an inefficiency, are much more receptive to discussing it than the individuals who are not and, in fact, may be the cause of the problem.

is a declaration of certainty. The salesperson is certain that his solution will be valuable to the prospective customer, just as it has been of value to others, and he or she says something like, "May I show you how our solution will improve your business?" The problem with a question like this is that it challenges or provokes the customer, who immediately thinks or says, "Sure it will. Prove it." The salesperson begins the initial approach in a defensive position.

A *value hypothesis*, in contrast, is based on facts about the customer company. The sales professional has noticed certain physical evidence, and in many cases, this evidence suggests that certain performance metrics within the customer's business could be at risk. Thus, the value hypothesis is really a question posed by the sales professional to the customer, such as, "Are you also seeing this evidence and does this degree of risk, relative to your other priorities, warrant taking the time to check the validity of the hypothesis?" It leads the executive to say, "Help me prove my performance is at risk." The power of the value hypothesis is that it sets up a relationship based on credible, open, and honest communication. It is an observation developed into a hypothesis, rather than a value assault, which is an unverified opinion or judgment about the customer's situation. The value hypothesis also sets up a collaborative conversation where both parties are looking to validate the hypothesis, whereas the value assault sets up the classic sales argument—salesperson presents, customer objects.

In the case of the circuit board equipment manufacturer described previously, the salesperson's value hypothesis, directed at the VP of sales, sounded something like this, "I've had a chance to talk with a few of your salespeople and they said they can't bid on jobs requiring components smaller than 9 microns. They helped me make a preliminary estimate and it looks like the lost opportunity could be around $8 million to $9 million. I'm wondering, based on all the other priorities you are dealing with, if it would make sense to look into this in more detail to see if that amount is valid and if so, determine if we could help you recover that revenue?"

As the example suggests, you should direct your value hypothesis at the executive who is the ultimate victim in the absence of your value. This executive should recognize the value hypothesis as relevant, and should become your sponsor in the sales engagement. In fact, once the executive decides that the hypothesis is likely to be true, he or she will have already taken the first step on the *Bridge to Change*.

How to Be Invited In

Once you have identified the individual who represents the best point of entry to a potential customer and created your value hypothesis, it is time to initiate the first formal contact. Many books have been written about this initial contact. They cover telephone skills and conversational gambits aimed at one thing—getting the appointment. Unfortunately, most miss the most important consideration in the initial customer contact.

The most successful sales professionals think beyond simply setting the appointment. Their goal in the initial conversation is to determine whether this prospective customer represents the best place that they can be at this time. The more resources that a sales engagement requires, the more scrutiny they devote to crafting and delivering this conversation. They want to get invited into the right customer's organization by the right people for the right reasons.

You don't need to read a shelf of books to discover the real secret to "getting invited in." It isn't that complicated. *In approaching your first conversation, you should orient everything you say to the customer's perspective and focus the entire content of your call exclusively on the customer's situation.* The most successful sales professionals don't initiate contact by talking at length about their company, their offering, or themselves. They introduce and describe themselves through the issues that they address, not through the solutions they offer. As I said earlier, this is called *diagnostic positioning*.

Any time a prospective customer takes a call and speaks to a salesperson for the first time, the customer is seeking answers to a short list of questions. The questions that customers ask themselves are simple, and the answers they infer are considered from only one point of view—their own:

- Should I talk with this person?
- Is this call relevant to my situation?
- Is this something we should discuss further?

The key to being "invited in" at the conclusion of the call is in offering customers the information that they need to answer each question—no more and no less. If the customer is able to answer questions in a positive way, the result is continued interaction. If not, the conversation is over.

To talk or not to talk? That is the question and the starting point of all conversations. It's a basic decision, and its answer is determined on basic information. You know what makes you decide not to talk—the mispronounced name, the rapid-fire delivery, and the obvious use of a script.

Now, consider the things that compel you to stay on the line with a salesperson. Certainly, the sound of the salesperson's voice is one. Does this person have a professional tone that is relaxed and unrushed? What about the introductory statements callers use? Does the caller introduce himself and say your name? Has the caller been referred by someone you know? Is the caller talking to you or reading from a page? Does the caller suggest that the conversation that is about to ensue may not be appropriate and ask you to decide if it is? Asking customers to decide if a call is appropriate (something that they will do whether you ask or not) is a powerful conversational tool.[2] It immediately relaxes customers and actually begins the conversation with agreement. It also suggests that you will not pressure them if they feel that there is no value to be gained in the conversation.

All of this adds up to a single judgment in the customer's mind: does this caller sound and act like a professional, like a colleague? When we sound professional, customers stay on the line. When we don't, they don't.

The next question that customers consider is whether the call is relevant to their current situation. Customers want to know if we understand their world and, at this point, we need to establish that we do. Here, the best sales professionals begin to demonstrate the knowledge they have obtained about the customer's industry, company, and business conditions. If you were in the customer's shoes, you would want to know whether the caller typically works with (as opposed to sells to) people like you. What kinds of issues do the salesperson's solutions typically connect to? Do these issues concern the customer? Once this information is communicated, the customer is ready to make the final decision in the initial contact.

The final question that customers consider is whether the initial contact should be extended to another call or a meeting. They are trying to figure out if this salesperson can add to their understanding of the problem at hand. The customer often asks questions such as, "How can you help me?" At this point, conventional salespeople are very happy to begin presenting their solutions, but the best sales professionals take a step back. Instead, they begin to describe the diagnostic process through which they will guide the customer, and they begin to establish the ground rules for further engagement.

The Diagnostic Agreement for Privileged Access and Insight

The final task of the Discover phase is the establishment of a *diagnostic agreement*. Diagnostic agreements are informal, verbal agreements between the sales professional and the customer. They lay out the ground rules for a constructive sales engagement.

These agreements lay the foundation for the beginning of the Diagnose phase of the Prime Process. They also set a professional tone for the continued conversations between the salesperson and the customer and set the stage for open communication. This is accomplished by setting limits on future conversations, thus assuring customers that they will not be forced into situations in which they are not comfortable.

The effective diagnostic agreement explicitly defines parameters for continued conversations, a proposed agenda, the participants, and feedback plans. It sets up the flow of the diagnostic process that will follow and specifies individuals who should be involved and topics to be covered.

It also specifies mutual preparation that will be required to begin the next phase of the Prime Process. This preparation usually includes the facts and figures needed to check for symptoms of the customer's problem, the information and resources that the customer will bring to the next meeting, and the information and resources that the salesperson will bring.

The idea of mutual preparation is unique in a sales world where getting in the door is usually considered the ultimate goal of the first contact, but it is a standard feature in other professions, such as law, medicine, and consulting. When we ask customers to prepare for the next meeting, they begin to think about their situations, the specific symptoms of their problems, and the consequences and costs of their problems. We involve them ahead of the diagnosis, and we signal our intent to discuss their situation in greater depth and more detail.

After the salesperson and the customer agree on a value hypothesis and create a diagnostic agreement, the Discover phase is complete. Sales professionals know that they are spending their time and energy in the right place, and customers know that they are dealing with someone who can be trusted and will treat them with respect. The stage is set for the second phase of the Prime Process: Diagnose.

Diagnose Complex Problems

The Ultimate Source of Credibility and Differentiation

The core competency of the complex sale is the sales professional's ability to perform as an expert diagnostician. This diagnostic expertise enables us to help customers analyze and understand the causes, consequences, and costs of the problems they face or the opportunities they may be missing, a critical prerequisite of making a quality decision. Equally important, it allows us to shift the emphasis of the customer engagement from our solutions to their situations and their objectives, a shift that differentiates us from our competitors, creates significant customer comprehension, and builds the trust and credibility with which our customers perceive us. Even more important, it creates the incentive to change in customers' minds.

These outcomes stand in stark contrast to the activities of conventional sales processes, which, if you will remember, require that customers understand and communicate their problems to salespeople. Popular and widely accepted selling strategies and techniques, such as consultative selling, solution selling, needs analysis, and value messaging, all depend to a large degree on the customer's ability to self-diagnose and self-prescribe, an expertise that is in exceedingly short supply.

The assumption that customers can and should be diagnosing themselves causes further damage when salespeople, thinking that their customers clearly understand their problems and the need to resolve them, prematurely focus on presenting their solutions. Presenting solutions without connecting and quantifying their value merely creates intellectual interest and curiosity among customers, not the level of clarity required to drive change. As a result, the conventional salesperson wastes time and effort on the intellectually curious customer, while the economically serious customer, who is actually experiencing the symptoms and consequences of the absence of the solution's value, stands by unrecognized and unattended.

Conversely, when sales professionals in a diagnostic mode engage with customers, they are dealing directly with customers' realities—that is, what customers have experienced in the past, are currently experiencing, or will be exposed to in the future. Sometimes customers are aware of their problems, but frequently, especially as problems become more complex, they are unaware that they are at risk. Regardless, it is the goal of the Diagnose phase to help them fully realize their past, current, and future realities.

As we discussed in Chapter 3, when customers realize that they are dealing with real problems and real costs (as opposed to generic benefits), the urgency needed to drive the decision to change is created. They find themselves on the critical, actionable end of the change progression. In short, diagnosis, as it methodically uncovers evidence of serious risk and expands the customer's awareness, causes the customer to move along the *Progression to Change*.

A Wellspring of Exceptional Credibility

The ability to diagnose customer situations sets the best sales professionals apart from their competitors. Most salespeople devote themselves to establishing *expected credibility*. Typically, these salespeople establish expected credibility with customers by presenting information about their companies' brands, histories, success stories, and reputations. The irony of this approach is that it makes salespeople all sound the same. I always ask the participants in our seminars how much their "credibility" stories differ from their top competitors' stories. Most somberly admit that there really are not very many significant differences.

The ability to conduct a quality diagnosis can differentiate you from your competitors. It gives you another opportunity to establish *exceptional credibility* in your customers' eyes. The quest for exceptional credibility in the Diagnose phase of the Prime Process is undertaken in two essential ways.

The first is by uncovering the realities of the customers' environment and the problems and/or the risks they face in pursuit of their objectives. The best sales professionals will not recommend a solution without first confirming that the customer is actually experiencing the consequences of the problem that it is meant to solve, or is poised to capitalize on the opportunity the solution represents.

The second way, which is just as important, is by making sure that the customer fully and accurately perceives all ramifications of the problem. The decision to buy is the customer's decision, and the only way to ensure the quality of that decision is to ensure that customers are clear about the consequences and/or risks they will incur if they do not change.

In this sense, the objective of the sales professional is very much like the objective of the psychiatrist. An experienced psychiatrist may be able to diagnose a patient's mental illness after a single visit. After all, the doctor has treated many other patients who suffer from the same condition. Yet, it almost always takes several sessions before the patient believes he or she has a problem and believes that the doctor also understands that problem. Psychiatrists know that until patients come to those realizations, they will have difficulty establishing credibility and trust in patients' eyes, and the path to a cure will remain blocked.

When salespeople fail to properly diagnose customers' problems and ensure that customers thoroughly understand the risks they face, they fail to achieve exceptional credibility, and their ability to win complex sales is severely compromised. The outcome of the sale becomes random and unpredictable. When they don't thoroughly diagnose a complex problem, they have no basis for designing and delivering a high-quality solution. Additionally, if they diagnose complex problems, but don't help their customers to fully comprehend them, the customers will not see the need for change and will not buy.

The data and other information that sales professionals need to make an accurate diagnosis comes primarily from individuals within the customer's organization. Thus, the ability of sales professionals to ask highly effective questions of the right people becomes another essential source of credibility and differentiation, as well as the primary skill of the information-gathering process. The value of asking questions is also predicated on another important skill—listening. As noted doctor and author Oliver Sacks states, "There is one cardinal rule: One must always listen to the patient."[1]

Key Thought
You Gain More Credibility through the Questions You Ask Than the Stories You Tell.

Conventional salespeople tell stories about their solutions in an attempt to communicate value. Prospective customers expect to hear these stories and rarely take them seriously. What is taken seriously is the concern and expertise that we display in the questions we ask our customers. The right questions form the basis for customer opinions concerning how well salespeople understand customers' problems, whether they can help customers expand their own knowledge of the problems, and how likely they are to be the best source for the solution. The most compelling source of credibility is asking questions of your customers that your customers have not thought to ask themselves.

Questions are more than tools to elicit information. When questions are being asked and answered, the customer is forming opinions that are critical to the outcome of the decision/sale. The best sales professionals are guiding their customers to three fundamental decisions in the Diagnose phase. They are deciding:

1. Is this an issue that is affecting performance?
2. If so, what is its financial impact?
3. Is the financial impact great enough to proceed in search of a solution?

When we help our customers successfully navigate these decisions, it is highly likely that we have earned exceptional credibility in their eyes and have stepped into their world as a full-fledged business partner and a source of business advantage.

Next let's take a closer look at how Prime sales professionals help customers make these decisions.

Establishing the Critical Perspective

In the complex sale, the most successful sales professionals are seen by customers as valued business advisors and key contributors to their businesses. One of the ways they earn this distinction is by their ability to work with multiple individuals in the customer's organization to develop a comprehensive view of the situation. Each of these individuals has some of the information needed to diagnose the problem, and each has a unique perspective.

The Mayo Clinic, which *U.S. News & World Report* ranked second among almost 5,000 hospitals in its 2009–2010 America's Best Hospitals list, knows the power of perspective.[2] One of the ways in which this healthcare provider achieves this high level of care is by using a team-based approach to diagnosis. It brings various medical specialists together, each provides his or her view of the patient, and together they reach a consensus opinion.

The best salespeople approach the diagnosis of customer problems in much the same way: They seek to understand the perspectives of individuals with information about the customer's situation and weave that information together to create an accurate, holistic view.

To communicate most effectively with each of the individuals who has information about a complex problem, to obtain the best information they have to offer, and to evaluate the validity of that information, you must first consider the *critical perspective* of each person—that is, the mind-set and position from which each of them is seeing the symptoms of the problem.

There are three questions that you can ask to understand a person's critical perspective:

1. *What is this person's education and career background?* In Chapter 4, I talked about how the background of an organization's leaders can affect the way the entire organization thinks. So, too, the background of an individual colors his or her personal perspective of the world. For instance, a person with an education in accounting approaches and perceives a problem differently than a person educated in marketing.

2. *What are this person's job responsibilities?* An individual's critical perspective is going to be intimately linked with his or her current goals and duties. Certainly, personal concerns about job security and performance are among the most powerful forces at work on the change spectrum.

3. *What are the performance issues that concern this person?*
   We often find salespeople trying to engage customers
   in issues and problems that exist outside an individual's
   area of responsibility. For instance, a director of quality who is charged with maintaining unit defects at
   a consistent Six-Sigma level perceives an innovative
   new solution for speeding the manufacturing process
   from a very different perspective than a plant manager
   who is charged with obtaining higher output. The
   former will likely be thrilled with the status quo (if it
   has reached Six Sigma) and highly resistant to any
   change that could threaten it, while the latter sees the
   status quo as a performance problem that must be
   addressed.

A good way to begin answering these questions and
understanding the critical perspective of an individual
within a customer company is by asking yourself about
the typical concerns of individuals with this particular
job title. The director of quality is concerned with issues
such as product defects, process reliability, and customer
satisfaction. However, as soon as you get face-to-face with
this person, you must establish his or her critical perspective quickly, confirm the existence of those concerns, and
narrow your focus on the person's specific areas of
dissatisfaction.

To accomplish this, conventional approaches to selling usually depend on laundry lists of questions that focus
on customer needs and solutions. The disadvantage of
this process is that the salesperson may not begin to gain
insight into the customer's perspective and concerns until a
dozen or more questions have been asked, long after the
customer's patience has worn thin. In the Diagnose phase
of the Prime Process, we avoid this by using the A-to-Z
question (introduced in Chapter 3).

An A-to-Z question is designed to instantly bring to the surface the customer's most serious concern. Assume that you are a sales executive who has contacted me about my company's services. I'll ask you a question and you think about how you would answer it. Here goes:

> *As you consider your sales process and your responsibilities within it . . . starting with generating a new high-quality lead . . . moving on through all the interactions with a customer . . . and finally, ending up with a very successful customer and a profitable new account . . . if you had to choose one part of the entire sales process that concerns you the most . . . as well as things are going for you . . . what concern would you put at the top of your list?*

Let's table your answer for a moment and look at the question more closely. Note that it is a long question, and imagine me asking it with plenty of pauses and a long thoughtful look or two at the ceiling, which makes it even longer. There is good reason for that. I am trying to pace your thought process, and I'm giving you time to create a thoughtful response. Further, it sounds spontaneous, doesn't it? Not like the typical pre-scripted sales question at all.

Now, consider the content of the question. Note that it is designed to direct your thinking to a certain process within your job responsibility. Its goal is to create a picture of a current or past situation in your mind and provide you a frame for a meaningful response.

There is one more important element of the question that I'd like to point out—the phrase "as well as things are going for you." This is included to defuse any defensiveness you might be feeling. Without a phrase like this, many people would simply answer: "Things are going quite well, thank you." By acknowledging and complimenting your success, I am not attacking you at all. I am only suggesting that you might be interested in getting even better.

Now, consider your answer. Did you think about the question? Did it trigger a review of your sales process? Did you believe that the question was sincere and try to address it seriously? Most people do. In fact, after I ask A-to-Z questions, I always stop and just listen, even when the customer doesn't respond right away. Silence is good. The longer the silence lasts, the better the answer will be. The A-to-Z question is a most effective means of getting to customers' critical perspectives.

Peeling the Onion

In a perfect world, salespeople and their customers would communicate openly, honestly, and with complete clarity about the problems the customer is experiencing. But it's not a perfect world. In the real world of complex sales, customers are often unaware of the full extent of their problems; and even when they do understand them, they are just as often reluctant to share that information. People don't usually ask what they really want to know first, and they don't usually say what they really mean first. This lack of openness, which we all exhibit to one degree or another, is a natural and common protective behavior.

When sales professionals align their questions with the critical perspective of their customers, they begin to overcome the barriers to communication. Empathy, however, is not enough. Our customers need to be assured that it is safe to share information with us and that we will not use the information they provide to manipulate them. I've already discussed the first way we can communicate that assurance: by our willingness to walk away from an engagement whenever the facts dictate that there is no fit between the customer's situation and our offerings.

The second way we can assure our customers that we can be trusted is to approach the diagnosis at the customer's pace. Leading a witness is forbidden in a courtroom and should also be forbidden in the complex sale. Customers must discover, understand the impact of, and take ownership of problems before deciding to seek a solution. Yet, customers seldom reach conclusions about their problems at the same time that salespeople do. When salespeople move too quickly and too far ahead of their customers, they create a gap that customers often perceive as pressure or manipulation. The result is mistrust and a confrontational atmosphere.

Crossing customers' emotional barriers to get to the heart of the issues that concern them is like peeling an onion. When the most successful sales professionals peel the onion, they accomplish two goals: encouraging open communication and getting to the heart of problems.

Encouraging Open Communication

First, they pass through the layers of protection that customers use to shield themselves from the potentially negative impact of open communication. The best salespeople move from the realm of cliché (which is the surface level of emotion) through levels of fact and opinion to the most powerful driver of change—the urgency that is produced by the physical evidence of their customers' problems.

We peel the onion using a series of deliberately structured questions. This sequence of questions is based on the decision tree that I introduced in Chapter 3; it is also called a *diagnostic map*. Too often, salespeople ask questions simply to prolong conversations until they can create an opening to present their solutions. The result is surface communication and superficial engagement. A diagnostic map, on the other hand, enables them to explore issues in an accurate and efficient way while creating the trust needed to elicit forthright answers from our customers.

Assumptive questions are an excellent tool for moving through customers' protective layers and the diagnostic map. I've named them assumptive because they are always phrased in a way that assumes the customer is capable and knowledgeable, and has already considered the question. This phrasing is very important: It communicates respect for the customer and engenders customer trust.

Key Thought
The Three Most Important Words in Communication:
Nurture, Nurture, and Nurture.

People reveal their true feelings and problems only when they believe that their input will be respected and no negative consequences will result from the information they share. Prime salespeople are careful to communicate by word and deed that they mean customers no harm. This nurturing attitude enables open communication, mutual understanding, and maximizes the probability of a quality decision.

I once worked with a company that sells disaster recovery software. Its salespeople were using a slide-based presentation designed to educate the leaders of small- and mid-sized companies about the risks they were incurring without this software. One slide boldly stated: "Eighty percent of companies under $50M in sales do not have disaster recovery systems." When this slide appeared, the salespeople were supposed to read it aloud, pause, and then ask, "Do you?" This approach is straight out of the Era 1 playbook of present, intimidate, and manipulate. If you were the customer confronted with such a question, a question that infers that you have entirely overlooked a critical issue that could force your company to close its doors, how would you react? It is highly likely that you would become defensive and start listing the many good reasons why you haven't worked on it and why you won't be looking at it now.

By this point, it shouldn't come as any surprise to hear that I suggested to the company that it drop this one-sided and confrontational approach and replace it with a diagnostic conversation, including this assumptive question designed to address the same situation: *"When you put together your disaster recovery plan, which of the potential bottlenecks gave you the most concern?"* This implies that the customer knows his or her business, and because it assumes the best, the customer is complimented by that assumption and feels safe enough to admit it when there is no plan in place. It has the added benefit of introducing the idea that even if the company has a plan in place, it might not be comprehensive and the company might be exposed to other serious, and thus far, unaddressed, risks. On hearing the assumptive question, customers go through a sequence of thoughts: (1) feeling complimented; (2) realizing they either haven't considered the issue at all, or as fully as they could; and (3) recognizing the sales professional has added considerable value by introducing a topic that should not be overlooked. It creates trust of the sales professional, concern, and immediately establishes the sales professional as a valued business advisor who is qualified to assist in making this decision. A different form of a question can sometimes make all the difference. Not all questions are created equal!

Getting to the Heart of the Problem

The second goal of peeling the onion is to establish the existence and extent of the problem itself. Again, questions play the starring role in this work. A second type of question, the *indicator question*, is used to identify the symptoms or physical evidence of the kinds of problems our offerings are designed to solve. An indicator is a physical signal. It is a recognizable event, occurrence, or situation that can be seen, heard, or perceived by the customer. It doesn't require an expert opinion, and we are not asking the customer to self-diagnose. Instead, we are simply asking for an observation.

The difference between opinion and observation is important; the easiest way to make it clear is to look to the medical profession. Doctors don't ask patients for expert opinions. They don't put much value in patients' opinions, but they do value patients' observations. They ask indicator questions, such as, "Have you noticed any shortness of breath lately?" and "Have you experienced any dizziness or numbness?" These questions ask the patient for an observation and they lead to additional questions and a more in-depth diagnosis. The best salespeople ask the same kinds of questions.

> **Key Thought**
> **No Evidence—No Problem**
> **No Problem—No Change**
> **No Change—No Sale**
>
> The salespeople who attend our seminars often ask me what to do if they ask indicator questions and find no evidence that a customer company is at risk. My answer is simple: Leave.
>
> *(continued)*

(*continued*)

If there are no indicators, there is no problem. No problem means no incentive to change. Thus, the probability that the customer will make a decision to change is very low. The engagement is over or, at least, any further diagnosis should be postponed until such indicators appear. It is time to move this customer into your opportunity management system for future consideration and engage new customers who are experiencing the indicators of the problems you solve today.

Think of yourself as the doctor who finds no symptoms of a health risk or disease during a patient's annual physical. You wouldn't recommend surgery and the patient certainly wouldn't agree to it. However, you would note any symptoms on the patient's chart, suggest the patient pay attention to them, and schedule an appropriate time to re-examine them.

When indicators are present, we continue the questioning process to expand our own—and the customer's—understanding of the problem. We continue peeling the onion and exposing the full dimensions of the problem by creating sequences of linked questions. We link questions by building each new question on the customer's answer to the previous question. When we do this, we are encouraging further explanation and additional detail. Communications experts tell us that humans have a natural desire to be understood. With each new question, we tap into that desire in our customers, and together we reach a deeper understanding and a greater level of clarity about the problem.

Another tool for drilling deeper into problems and tapping into the customer's desire to be understood is a question called the *conversation expander*. Like indicator questions, these questions give our customers the opportunity to expand

Conversation Expanders

Indicator Expansion

Could you expand a bit on . . . ?
Tell me more about . . .
You mentioned a concern about . . . Could you walk me through that?
Could you help me understand . . . ?

Example of Situation

What would be an example of . . . ?
Could you give me an example of . . . ?
What would an example of . . . look like in your business/industry?
I'm not clear how . . . works. Can you give me an example?

Duration

When did you first start to experience . . . ?
When did you first notice . . . ?
Has . . . been happening for long?
How often does . . . happen?

FIGURE 5.1 Conversation Expanders

on explanations and clarify their thoughts. We can ask them at any stage of the Prime Process. Examples for using them during the Diagnosis phase are shown in Figure 5.1.

* * *

We ask diagnostic questions to locate tangible evidence that the links comprising a *chain of causality* actually exist. Indicators represent the symptoms of a problem, but symptoms represent only clues to actual causes of a problem. As any doctor will tell you, eliminating the symptoms of a problem does not solve the problem. For instance, a patient may use an antacid to ease the pain caused by an ulcer, but the antacid does not cure the ulcer nor does it address the causes of the ulcer. In fact, eliminating symptoms often masks the problem, enabling the problem to continue undetected, and sometimes even exacerbating it.

We identify the causes of problems by asking questions about their physical indicators. When we have uncovered physical evidence that the value we provide can have a significant impact on the customer's performance, we have also reached the causes of the customer's dissatisfaction. That dissatisfaction is the vehicle that drives the decision to change, but simply establishing the existence of a problem is not a complete diagnosis. A full diagnosis must include cost.

Establishing the Cost of the Problem

Salespeople can do a thorough job of establishing and communicating the symptoms and causes of customers' problems, present viable solutions to those problems, and still walk away from the engagement empty-handed. This outcome most often occurs when salespeople ignore a crucial piece of the diagnostic process—connecting a dollar value to the consequences of the problem.

Problems run rampant in all organizations. Some are not significant enough in terms of consequences and risks to address; others must be addressed because their consequences and risks are too high. The fact that a problem exists is not enough to ensure change. When the customer does not know the actual cost of a problem, the success of winning the complex sale is severely compromised.

Typically, customers cannot quantify the costs of complex problems on their own. The main reason for this, as described in Chapter 2, is that most customers simply don't have the expertise required to identify and calculate those costs. Even when they do attempt to quantify their problems, they usually focus on the surface costs and tend to overlook the total cost.

Key Thought
Pain Is the Vehicle That Drives the Sale, and the Cost of the Pain Is the Accelerator!

When we define the cost of the problem, we put a price tag on the dissatisfaction customers are experiencing.

That price tag enables customers to prioritize the problem and then make a rational, informed choice between continuing to incur its cost and investing in a solution. In fact, as we see in the next chapter, establishing an accurate cost of the problem is the only path to defining the true value of a solution. Cost is also the surest way to shorten the customer's decision cycle. Think of the customer's pain as the decision driver and the cost of the pain as its accelerator. The higher the cost of the problem, the faster the decision will be made to solve it.

Salespeople tend to shy away from quantifying the actual financial impact of their customers' problems. Sometimes they honestly believe this work is the customer's responsibility and that their customers don't need help to understand financial impacts—this is, after all, the common underlying assumption of the Era 2 sales processes they are taught to use.

Many other salespeople complain that it is too difficult to uncover financial impact and quantify the value. They base this conclusion on their experiences asking customers about costs. However, they typically ask cost questions that encompass too many elements. You know this is happening when customers respond by saying, "That's a tough question; that would be really hard to determine." The real problem is not that the cost is too difficult to quantify, but rather that salespeople do not have a proper formula for calculating it. The number one reason salespeople avoid quantifying their value is that they have not been equipped by their companies to do so.

The best sales professionals embrace the measurement of value and realize that the starting point for determining value is calculating the cost of the problem. They know that there is always the possibility that the cost of a problem will not be large enough to motivate the customer to change. They also know that such an outcome is entirely legitimate. If the cost of a customer's problem does not justify the solutions being offered, the professional will acknowledge that reality and, in the spirit of *always be leaving*, move on to a better qualified customer. (Of course, if this happens too often, salespeople and their organizations might very well have a larger problem. Their solutions may be too expensive in terms of the value they offer customers.)

Another common objection to the cost of the problem calculation that I hear from salespeople is that their offerings are not meant to solve problems. They tell me that their solution creates new opportunities for their customer; therefore, there is no problem to fix a cost to. This is not a valid position. If something is happening in a business, it can be measured in financial terms. There are risks and costs present in every decision. Even when a solution offers a new capability, there is still a cost if the customer chooses not to adopt it. It is the cost *incurred in the absence of the value your solutions provide*.

Key Thought
If You Don't Have a Cost of the Problem,
You Don't Have a Problem.

All businesses measure their performance in profit and loss; therefore, any problem they are experiencing, or opportunity they are missing, must be expressed in financial terms. Until you quantify that impact, you are dealing with a highly speculative issue.

When salespeople seek to establish the *total cost* of a problem, they need to use a combination of three types of figures:

1. *Direct numbers:* Established or known figures
2. *Indirect numbers:* Inferred or estimated figures
3. *Lost opportunities:* Figures representing the options that customers cannot pursue because of the resources consumed by the problem

When I talk about the total cost of the problem, I am not saying that you must establish a precise figure. Rather, the resulting number must be believed by the customer. This requires that the customer recognizes that the formula you provide is valid, and when used with the customer's numbers, will provide a credible outcome, that the customer is part of the calculation process, and that the customer is willing to "own" the outcome.

With these prerequisites in mind, calculating financial impact is a process similar to the navigational method known as triangulation. By sighting off of three points—direct numbers, indirect numbers, and lost opportunities—you can arrive at a financial impact that is believable to your customer (see Figure 5.2).

This is accomplished in two steps. First, we need to provide a formula that is conceptually sound. Second, we must ensure that the numbers plugged into that formula are derived from the customer's reality, not industry averages, past experiences with other customers, or other more questionable sources. We know we have successfully completed these steps when our customers are willing to defend the validity of the cost among their own colleagues.

Let's take a look at how a cost of the problem conversation should go. This is based on a cost of the problem

Cost of the Problem

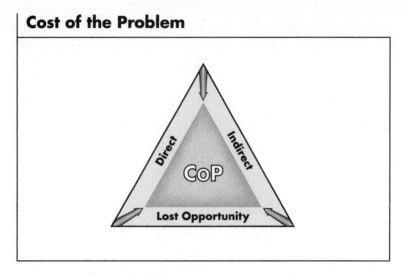

FIGURE 5.2   Cost of the Problem

conversation we designed for one of our client companies, a provider of shoplifting detection equipment to drugstores, which was finding it difficult to sell to stores in affluent communities.

The sales professional engages the manager of a drugstore with revenues of $1.5 million, who is experiencing the industry average inventory shrinkage of 3 percent. This tells the salesperson that the store is losing $45,000 annually to some combination of customer theft, employee theft, and/or sloppy inventory management. The manager, however, does not believe that the store is experiencing any significant customer theft because the store is in a "better part of town," and therefore, is not interested in the salesperson's detection equipment.

The salesperson agrees with the customer (creating an atmosphere of cooperation), and then asks an indicator question, "Do you ever notice empty packages on the floor?" The store owner replies, "You have a point there, but it's not enough to be worried about." "Probably not," the salesperson replies, and then asks the next question to establish an indirect number. "Out of every 100 people in this community, how many do you think would shoplift?" The now-curious owner replies, "Oh, I suppose one percent, 1 out of 100."

The salesperson now asks for two direct numbers—the average sales per day ($4,100) and the amount of the average sale ($16). This yields the number of buying customers (257). He then asks the manager for an indirect number— the number of browsers in the store who don't buy. The manager says. "About the same number as those who buy." That yields a figure of 514 people in the store each day. The salesperson then asks for another indirect number: "What do you think the average loss from a shoplifting incident would be?" The manager replies, "$15 to $20."

From this information, the salesperson calculates that there are approximately five (1 out of 100) shoplifters in the store each day and the average daily loss is $75 ($15 × 5). Further, the store is open 365 days each year, making the annual loss $27,000—a believable figure in light of the store's $45,000 annual shrinkage.

The detection equipment costs $12,000 to install and $2,000 per year for activated price tags. Subtracted from the cost of the store's problem, this yields a positive return of $13,000 the first year and $25,000 in subsequent years. Over three years, the lost opportunity is $20,000 per year.

This example is a condensed version of an actual sales engagement drawn from our client files. The salesperson made his initial contact, taking a compelling value hypothesis to the CFO of a national retail chain. He set up a diagnostic agreement with the CFO, his executive sponsor, to visit several of the chain's locations, and held similar cost of the problem conversations with the store managers in each location. Then, he returned to the CFO, described his findings, and extrapolated them for the entire chain. He won a contract to install his company's equipment in the chain's stores nationwide.

It's worth noting that the security director of the drugstore chain was not interested in buying the shoplifting detection equipment. He thought it was too expensive and not that effective. It was the CFO who was the ultimate victim of the absence of value. He pinpointed a lost opportunity cost when he said, "If I can get $20,000 back from each installed system, I can fund a new store per year for every ten systems."

As you can see, you can determine the financial impact of a problem in much the same way as you explore other aspects of customers' situations. You use a structured approach and diagnostic questioning. The answers to these cost-related questions tell you whether customers have the resources and are willing to solve their problems. More importantly, the process of answering questions allows customers to reach their own conclusions in their own time. Further, the fact that the customer provides the data enhances the credibility of the resulting cost conclusions. This creates a high level of buy-in. This process is far more compelling and accurate than the generic cost/return formulas and average industry costs that salespeople so often use in conventional presentations.

The cost of the problem formula is a critical component of the quality decision process that you bring to your customer. Customers do not have the expertise or the inclination to put such a formula together on their own; however, if you provide it, you will clearly differentiate yourself from your competitors in your customers' eyes.

Determine the Priority to Act

The final element of the Diagnose phase is to determine the problem's priority in the customer's mind. This is one crucial test of a problem's consequences and the customer's incentive to change that salespeople often overlook. The fact that the cost of the problem is substantial in the salesperson's eyes in no way guarantees that the customer feels the same way or has any inclination to resolve the problem.

There are two very good reasons for this. First, it is entirely possible that the cost is an accepted part of doing business. A retail chain includes a line item for inventory shrinkage in its annual budget; a manufacturing plant considers some level of defects acceptable. Unless the cost exceeds acceptable levels, salespeople may well find that the customer will not feel the need to make a decision to change. Second, even when costs do exceed acceptable levels, they may not be compelling in light of the other critical issues vying for the resources of the organization. If, for example, a customer is confronting issues or objectives with larger financial impacts, it would be the right business decision to pursue those opportunities first. If that is the case, the most credible position you can take is to support the customer's priorities rather than argue about them, and determine when the issue your solution addresses will rise to the top of the customer's priority list. This is why it is so important to ask the customer to prioritize the problem and its costs before moving out of the Diagnose phase of the Prime Process. Again, this information is developed by asking questions, such as conversation expanders (see Figure 5.3).

The Buying Decision

My discussion of the Diagnose phase is now complete and I'd like to take a moment to review what the best sales professionals accomplish when they execute it well.

Conversation Expanders: Cost of the Problem

Cost Quantification

Have you had a chance to put a number on . . . ?
What does your experience tell you . . . is costing?
Can you give a ballpark number as to what . . . costs?

Cost Prioritization

How does . . . compare to other issues you are dealing with?
Does it make sense to go after a solution to . . . at this time?
When you consider all the issues on your desk, where does . . . fall?

FIGURE 5.3 Conversation Expanders: Cost of the Problem

- They help their customers realize that they are experiencing a condition that could be placing their personal and/or business objectives at risk.

- They assist their customers in conducting a thorough exploration of the dimensions of the problem and establish its financial impact—the cost of the problem.

- They work with customers to determine whether that cost justifies immediate action relative to other issues and opportunities.

If you are still engaged with the customer at this point in the Prime Process, it is for one reason only: *the customer has made the decision to change and has also decided that you have the credibility, and likely the solution, to facilitate that change.*

Think about that. You have not made a sales presentation. In fact, you haven't devoted any significant time to describing your solutions at all. You haven't exerted any pressure on the customer whatsoever. Nevertheless, the customer has decided there is a problem that is costing more than he or she is willing to absorb and that you, the salesperson, understand the situation. Invariably, the customer has also made a leap of logic and now assumes that because you have taken him or her this far through the decision process, you will also have a solution to the problem.

There are two conventional sales paradigm-busting realities that underlie these outcomes: First, customers don't need to have a solution in mind to determine that they have a problem. Second, customers don't need to have a solution in mind to decide to solve that problem. In fact, introducing solutions too early in the complex sale will frequently distract and confuse the customer—creating a barrier to effective diagnosis, creating uncertainty around the problem, and throwing the customer's decision process off track.

The key to managing the customer's decision process is staying true to the *Bridge to Change* decision sequence. You can gain the inside track on any sale by following that progression and helping your customers establish that:

- There is a problem and they are at risk.
- It is costing them a specific amount to leave that problem unattended.
- The amount it costs is significant enough to act on.

You entered the Diagnose stage with a value hypothesis that compelled your customer to work with you. You have now confirmed the risks in that hypothesis by finding physical evidence, connecting it to specific performance metrics, and collaboratively quantifying the financial impact on those metrics. You have reached the value-required stage of the Value Life Cycle. The customer requires value to solve the problem or address the situation. The incentive to change has been established.

At the same time that your customers have reached the *crisis* stage in the *Progression to Change*, you are establishing your own value in their eyes. You will have earned the respect of your customers because of your ability to conduct a high-quality diagnosis. You will have earned the trust of your customers because of your willingness to end the engagement at any time the diagnosis revealed that a problem did not exist or was not worth acting on. You will have created exceptional credibility by demonstrating an in-depth understanding of the customer's business. You really will be seen as a valued business advisor in the customer's eyes.

Now that the customer has made the decision to change, who do you think the customer believes is best qualified to help design a high-quality solution to the problem? Granted, customers may not openly announce that you are their first choice, but you will see it in their open and trusting demeanors. All the signs, such as the customer's willingness to answer questions and provide access to people and information, will verify the fact that the decision has been made. If you grab hold of this one idea—that the decision to buy is made during diagnosis as opposed to during the close—it will create a profound change in your results. Your days of *Dry Runs* will be over.

Key Thought
The Decision to Change, to Buy, and from Whom Is Made During the Diagnosis.

Conventional salespeople believe the decision to buy is made after they have presented the solution and as they are handling objections and attempting to close. One of the most significant paradigm shifts of the Prime Process is that as you conduct a thorough diagnosis, and by the time your customer has made the three elemental decisions of the Diagnose phase, it is highly likely that the customer has already made his or her decision to change—the decision to buy. Since you have established exceptional credibility, it is also highly likely the customer has decided to buy from you and your company. It is yours to lose.

Design the Value-Rich Solution

Creating the Confidence to Invest

In the Design phase of the Prime Process, the most effective sales professionals focus their efforts on defining solutions that will best accomplish their customers' business and personal objectives. They guide the Design process by aligning the expectations of the individuals within the cast of characters. In this phase, they are helping their customers to:

- Build consensus and confirmation among the cast of characters within the customer's organization based on findings and decisions that resulted from the diagnosis and design efforts
- Establish expectations about solution outcomes
- Determine the constraints in and around the customer's environment that may restrict or prevent the customer's ability to accomplish those outcomes
- Determine the methods and alternatives for obtaining those outcomes, including changes the customer needs to make in order to remove constraints and achieve the desired outcomes
- Determine the financial impact of the solution, investment levels, and implementation timing
- Define the criteria that will govern buying decisions

In reading these bulleted points, you probably noticed that they say nothing about the specific products and services that your company sells. Instead, they are entirely focused on helping customers understand the parameters of a high-quality solution and prepare to manage the risks of the change that they are considering. In terms of the

Value Life Cycle, the customer is clarifying the *value expected*, that is, the value that he or she will achieve as a result of implementing your solution. This, in turn, creates the confidence to invest, because the customer believes that the constraints to change will be dealt with, the risks of change have been minimized, and the desired results will be obtained.

In the Design phase, the most successful sales professionals are specifying and confirming the customer's preferred outcomes and decision-making criteria, but they are not presenting solutions. This is a continuation of the spirit of partnership and collaboration that the Prime Process is aimed at building throughout the sales engagement, and it further solidifies the sales professional's role as a trusted advisor in customers' minds.[1]

This third phase of the Prime Process stands in stark contrast to conventional selling processes. In conventional selling, the only acceptable result of an engagement is the customer buying the salesperson's offering. When salespeople enter the engagement, they always have this fixed end in mind. Regardless of the customer's situation and requirements, the salesperson who follows a conventional strategy is focused on only one solution—his or her own. Given this pre-established outcome, is it any wonder that so many customers perceive sales engagements as zero-sum games and think of salespeople as James or Jamie Bonds who are willing to use any means to achieve their ends?

The most successful sales professionals have no such preconceived notion in mind. They approach the Design phase of the complex sale as a collaborative process, whose aim is to equip the customer to make the best, most effective choice among the solutions competing in the marketplace. This is not to say that they approach an engagement without a *preferred* solution in mind. They are in business to sell their products and services. They understand, however, that their solutions are not always the best options for every customer, and they will only recommend their solutions if and when it is determined that they are in the best interests of their customers. As always, they apply the "do no harm" principle of the doctor and the integrity test of the best friend.

If these sales professionals' offerings do not provide meaningful value to the customer, they are the first to recognize and acknowledge that fact and even recommend a more appropriate source for the required solution. In this way, they protect and retain their "valued business advisor" status in the customer's mind and remain welcome to work with the customer at a future date. At the same time, the salesperson is free to move on to a more qualified customer.

While conventional salespeople often act as if competing solutions do not exist, the most successful sales professionals willingly discuss competing solution alternatives. They know that in the competitive environment of the complex sale, customers will examine alternative solutions with or without them, and they realize that actively participating in that examination is better than ignoring it. Given the fact that so many salespeople are afraid to acknowledge competing solutions, the customer-first, business advisor stance of the best sales professionals often becomes a positive differentiating factor in and of itself.

When salespeople act as business advisors and join the customer's search for the best solution, they take a seat on the same side of the table with the customer and behave like partners instead of adversaries. Further, they can use this opportunity to strengthen their position by ensuring that their customers fully recognize the inherent advantages and disadvantages among the solution alternatives.

Three Types of Solution Risk

One of the goals of the Design phase is to minimize the risk of change for the customer. In the Diagnose phase, we maximize the customer's awareness of risk. That is, we help them to fully comprehend the risk involved in not changing, be that not addressing their problems or not acting on an opportunity. When that effort is successful, customers are convinced that their decisions are sound and have the incentive to change.

In the Design phase, which the customer enters mentally prepared to make a change, we begin working to minimize the exposure to risk inherent in the act of changing. When this effort is successful, the customer will own the solution, clearly see how it will be successful for them, and have the confidence to invest.

Customers are exposed to three types of solution risks that you need to consider when designing solution parameters: process risk, performance risk, and personal risk.

- Process risks are exposures that stem from the implementation and ongoing operation of a solution.
- Performance risks are exposures that stem from the outcomes produced by a solution.
- Personal risks are exposures that the members of the cast of characters incur when they lend their personal support to a solution.

As we create and define the parameters of a high-quality solution, we need to anticipate how each of these three risks might impact the customer and be sure to communicate those exposures to the customer during the decision-making process.

To illustrate these risks, let's use financial accounting software as an example. A process risk associated with this software is the possibility that it could corrupt the organization's financial database. A performance risk is the possibility that the new software does not work and miscalculates the organization's financial results. A personal risk is the possibility that the problems that arise from purchasing the new software cause the person who recommended the purchase to be fired or shuffled off to a much less desirable job within the organization.

Now, consider the risks that a customer faces when buying your solution. What are the process, performance, and personal risks? How do you discuss and resolve them during the sales engagement?

Key Thought
There Are No Free Moves.

When it comes to making a decision to purchase a complex solution, no matter what solution the customer chooses, including your own, that solution will contain positive and negative aspects. Thus, there are consequences to every decision. When we willingly and openly explore alternative solutions and their ramifications from the customer's perspective, we exhibit integrity and strengthen the bonds of trust between our customers and ourselves.

Six Essential Design Questions

The focal point in the Design phase is on the customer's desired future state. For this reason, the process of Design is primarily a visioning process. We want to create and lead a discussion that is centered at a point in time when the customer's objectives have been achieved. This portrait of the future helps us define the customer's expectations about the solution. We can sum up these expectations in the answers to six questions.

The first three questions are focused on identifying the highest-value solution:

1. What business outcomes does the customer expect of the solution?
2. How can the customer achieve the outcomes?
3. What financial impact should the outcomes deliver?

The second three questions are focused on obtaining and capturing the value of the solution:

4. What level of investment is appropriate to achieve the desired outcome?
5. How soon does the customer need to see results?
6. How will the customer choose, implement, and measure the results of the solution?

These questions are purposefully sequenced such that each question, when answered, provides a solid foundation upon which to consider and answer the next question. Let's take a closer look at each one.

Expectations: What Business Outcomes Does the Customer Expect of the Solution?

The best way to begin to define the parameters of a solution is to ask customers how they expect their situation to look after the problem is solved. This imagined, and often idealized future yields a list of outcomes that customers expect from the solution. It also provides sales professionals with the basic information that they need to begin to define the standards by which those outcomes will be measured.

As always, questions are the most effective tool at our command. We use them to add depth to the customer's vision for solution outcomes. For instance, when a customer says that *reliability* is a critical outcome, it is our cue to ask questions that generate more clarity about that outcome. We need to establish an agreed definition of "reliability" and an exact figure for its measurement. In the process of establishing those answers, we are creating a clear definition of the customer's expectations and a valuable guide to the best solution to the customer's problem.

Key Thought
No Mind Reading: Clarify All Fat and Loaded Words.

"Reliability" is an example of what I call a fat or loaded word. So are words such as "quality," "value," "soon," and "support." Customers often use words like these to describe their expectations about solutions (as well as their problems), but the words themselves are vague and can easily cause misunderstandings. If your company's definition of quality is a 5 percent defect rate and your customer's definition is a 2 percent rate, and you don't uncover that discrepancy, you are setting yourself up for failure.

In addition to preventing miscommunication, sales professionals must ensure that the customer's requirements of a solution are realistic and attainable. Just because you ask customers to define their expectations does not necessarily mean that you should or can accept whatever answers they offer, or expect that your company can create and deliver a solution that can produce the outcomes that the customer is describing. The outcomes that customers envision must be possible, and it is your job to ensure that fact by managing the formulation process.

Mismatches between customer expectations and reality are a common occurrence, and too often salespeople abdicate responsibility for resolving them. Instead of bringing the customer back to earth as soon as unreasonable expectations surface, salespeople, who are almost always reluctant to say anything that might disappoint a customer, pass that unpleasant task downstream to the service and support functions. As a result, the customer's expectations become fixed, and when reality finally strikes, the level of dissatisfaction is higher. This also puts the seller's service and support staff in a very uncomfortable position. There is little point in providing a solution to a customer if we have fostered exaggerated expectations about performance of the product or service (or delivery date or final cost, for that matter). The only results we can expect from such a sale are complaints, conflict, negative press, and, in many cases, permanent loss of the customer.

Defining realistic expectations, on the other hand, builds trust and sets the stage for customer satisfaction and repeat and referral business. By defining expectations in quantitative as well as qualitative terms, we protect our customers and ourselves from disappointments and conflicts that result from poorly defined and unrealistic expectations.

Alternatives: How Can the Customer Achieve the Desired Outcome?

Once we have helped our customers create a portrait of what the desired outcome is going to look like, we need to turn our attention to the next set of solution parameters: how they will decide on the best solution alternative available to them. To do this, we create a set of guidelines by which customers can judge all solutions and the proof points needed to measure, analyze, and compare solution alternatives. This is where we arm customers with the questions they need to ask to clarify vague answers and avoid the smoke and mirrors that too often accompany complex solutions.

The truth is that alternatives always exist in the marketplace and each carries differing degrees of risk. The best sales professionals help customers recognize the consequences of their choices. This is very similar to the process that doctors go through when prescribing medications. In the United States, the Food and Drug Administration requires that every prescription drug carry with it a full description of contraindications, warnings, adverse reactions, possible side effects, and detailed instructions for proper dosage. Patients often ignore this "small print," but doctors use this very specific and detailed description to make informed decisions about prescribing a drug and communicating that choice to their patients.

The customer's awareness of alternatives and their consequences reinforces reasonable expectations, supports a high-quality choice of solution, and serves as the basis for monitoring the progress and adjusting solutions during implementation.

Taking an active hand in evaluating alternatives is a task that is largely nonexistent in conventional selling. Traditional salespeople depend on their customers to provide these criteria, and, as you already know, customers typically do not have the expertise to undertake this task. Further, conventional salespeople are often reluctant to admit the existence of alternative solutions that might compete with their own offerings. They are ignoring the reality that customers are going to be exposed to alternative solutions.

Conversely, the most successful sales professionals face the reality that the marketplace is a competitive arena and that their customers often have instant access to information about competing solutions. They know that their customers are going to explore these alternative solutions with or without them, and they understand that the only true choice salespeople have in the matter is whether to participate in that process. As always, and throughout the Prime Process, successful salespeople recognize that the most logical and credible approach is to help guide and shape the customer's decision process.

Alternative parameters specify the features, situations, and capabilities required to achieve the expectations of the customer. They are the material specifications of the customer's vision. They enable customers to explore treatment options in an organized fashion, ensure that alternatives are weighed equally, allow customers to match solutions to expectations, and then test and confirm their choices.

Alternative parameters are not a laundry list of features and benefits. In other words, salespeople can't simply cut and paste the capabilities of their offerings in this list. The parameters must grow from the expectations of the customer, and they must be directly connected to the findings of the Diagnose phase. When we specify a solution's capabilities within the alternative parameters, they must relate to a symptom or indicator of the problem and the costs associated with the problem. Otherwise, there is no defensible reason for requiring the capabilities of the solution.

This is a critical connection. How often have you had a customer become enamored with a competitor's product or service feature that sounds, looks, and smells good, but which the customer doesn't need? The customer is seduced by the decision principle: "If in doubt, it's better to have a feature than not have it." In this state, customers suddenly announce that they need a specific capability and they want to know if you have it.

For example, say the feature in question is a whicker attachment (an imaginary part) that your product does not include. A competitor has presented the whicker as the latest and greatest product feature, and now the customer wants a whicker attachment. How do you validate that requirement and address the customer's expectation? The alternative parameters tell us whether a whicker actually addresses an indicator present in the customer's problem or if it is a superfluous feature. (By the way, if the customer does actually need a whicker and we can't provide it, it may be time to consider the key thought, *always be leaving*.)

In complex sales, the list of alternative parameters can quickly get unwieldy. For this reason, I usually suggest that salespeople focus on a short list of three parameters that will have the most impact on an individual's decision. Within each of these three parameters, we need to teach our customers to ask the solution questions that make sense for their companies.

Consider a customer who is planning to buy capital equipment that requires authorized service to install it in plants in 21 countries around the world. Service support is obviously a critical issue in such a purchase. Typically, a customer in this situation asks: "Do you have a service program in place that will cover my 21 international plants?" The salesperson replies, "Of course, we offer a global service program." The customer checks off this need on his list and moves on.

What happens after the customer buys from this salesperson and the capital equipment installed in Singapore breaks down? The customer calls for service and finds out that it will be 48 hours before the service technician in London can get to Singapore. This creates two days of downtime before the technician even arrives on-site, and the customer is wondering how many days of downtime will be recorded when he starts multiplying the number by 21 countries.

The global service program that the salesperson promised actually means that his company will send a technician from its headquarters to wherever the equipment is located. However, the customer never discovered this shortcoming because he didn't think to ask the next logical questions: "Where are your service technicians located?" "How long will it take them to get to my sites?"

When sales professionals who are acting like valued business advisors help customers establish alternative parameters, they pay particular attention to those points where their product and service strengths intersect with the customer's expectations. Valuable opportunities to differentiate ourselves from our competitors exist at these points.

Key Thought
What Can Go Wrong Will Go Wrong.

The same concept that applies to medical prescriptions also applies to business solutions. To make a high-quality decision about solutions, the customer must be aware of the potential risk associated with available alternatives.

Financial Impact: What Return Should the Outcomes Deliver?

The next set of parameters we need to establish centers around quantifying the value of the solution. The level of financial analysis required to accomplish this is a significant portion of our work and beyond the scope of this book. However, it is important to understand what must be determined financially. In the Diagnose phase, we assigned a cost to the customer's current situation or cost of the problem (CoP). In the Design phase, we calculate the financial impact of the solution (FoS).

This does not mean that it is time to talk about the price of our solutions or to begin negotiating price with the customer. Instead, we are going to quantify the financial impact of the desired outcome, that is, what the customer can expect in terms of increased revenue and/or decreased expense. We want to determine what it is worth to the customer to solve the problem. The value of a solution and an appropriate investment to obtain it can be expressed with a simple equation:

$$\text{Financial impact of the solution (FoS)} - \\ \text{Cost of solution (CoS)} = \text{True value (value)}$$

Think of value as net profit to your customer. When customers know the financial impact of a solution, many of the price pressures that salespeople typically face disappear. In fact, the actual cost of the solution being offered becomes far less important than how that cost compares to the value the customer stands to gain. The ability to analyze value in this way is a significant improvement over the typical side-by-side price comparison of solutions that tell customers nothing about how much value each solution will create and therefore, nothing about what a realistic investment could be to solve the problem.

Investment Expectations: What Level of Investment Is Appropriate to Solve the Problem?

Once the value parameters are set, the next solution parameter is what level of investment makes business sense for the customer. This can also be expressed in a simple equation:

$$\text{Financial impact of the solution (FoS)}/$$
$$\text{Customer's required ROI (return on investment)}$$
$$= \text{Maximum investment}$$

Defining investment expectations is a boon to both the customer and the sales professional. The customer now knows how much to realistically invest in a solution. The sales professional now knows whether the solution is financially feasible for the customer. If it is feasible, the engagement continues. If not, the customer's expectations must be adjusted or the customer is returned to the salesperson's opportunity management system and it is time to move on to a more qualified customer. Also, setting investment expectations largely eliminates price negotiations and objections about the price of your offerings. You know ahead of time that the investment required to purchase your solutions is a match with the customer's expectations.

Conventional salespeople tend to accept customer budgets. In doing so, however, they are opening themselves up to three potential problems. First, the fact that a budget exists suggests that they are arriving late, and the later they arrive, the more difficult it is to establish accurate investment criteria. Second, an existing budget is a good indication that the customer is already working with a competitor, who is the likely source of the budget estimates. Third, because the budget is probably not an accurate reflection of the customer's requirements, it is unlikely to support the proper level of investment.

Timing: How Soon Does the Customer Need to See Results?

The next set of solution parameters is based on the timing of the expected outcomes. These are relatively simple to establish and don't require much explanation, but they

Key Thought
Budgets Are Not Cast in Stone.

Conventional selling puts great emphasis on the customer's budget. Budgets are part of the corporate planning process. They represent management's desire to forecast and assign resources for anticipated needs. Conventional sales methods ignore the reality that the corporate budget is largely irrelevant in the complex sale.

Value-laden purchases are investments. Corporate resources flow to the best investment, that is, the investment with the greatest potential return. When making quality business decisions, budgets are altered and created; they rarely impede an attractive investment. Our goal is to work with customers to create the investment criteria on which the budget is eventually based.

are important. After all, in today's fast-changing world, a solution that arrives late can cause as much damage as one that does not arrive at all.

The customer's expectations as to the timing of the solution tell us when the solution must be in place and the timetable by which it must be producing results. Further, timing parameters have the added benefit of signaling the customer's intentions for purchasing the solution, thus offering valuable information to the sales professional and another opportunity to influence the final decision.

As in establishing our customers' expectations about solution outcomes, it is our job to ensure that their timing expectations are clearly defined, mutually understood, reasonable, and attainable.

Decision Criteria: How Will the Customer Buy, Implement, and Measure the Results of the Solution?

During the Diagnose phase, the cast of characters within the customer company made four critical decisions:

1. They decided that the physical evidence of a problem or an unaddressed opportunity was compelling enough to quantify its impact.
2. They decided on the financial impact of their current situation.
3. They decided that the financial impact is unacceptable.
4. They decided to pursue a solution capable of addressing that impact.

By this point in the Design phase, the cast of characters in the customer company has made five critical decisions:

1. They have decided on realistic expectations for solution outcomes.
2. They have decided on a preferred approach to achieve their expectations.
3. They have decided on the value they should receive.
4. They have decided what they will invest to receive this value.
5. They have decided when they want the solution in place.

Now, the customer must determine the decision criteria for selecting a solution provider. These criteria provide the customer with a clear set of parameters for scrutinizing competing solution offerings in terms of how well each will achieve the customer's expectations.

The decision criteria have already been determined by the nine decisions mentioned previously as well as the exceptional levels of clarity and alignment you have helped your customer achieve. Thus, the customer is well situated to restate the previously mentioned decisions as firm criteria. The customer knows what to ask, what to measure, and what to compare as various solution providers are considered.

For example, because the customer has determined the consequences of his or her situation during the Diagnose phase, these consequences can now form the basis of their selection criteria. In other words, the customer adopts selection criteria that address and resolve each consequence.

* * *

The challenge of Era 3 is helping customers make high-quality decisions in their quest to solve complex problems and capture complex opportunities. By guiding your customers through the six Design questions, you have prepared them to find the best solutions and ask very precise questions that require very precise answers of potential suppliers. In doing so, you have implicitly shown that you have the answers that they are looking for, and even better yet, you have set a very high standard that your competitors must meet to win the sale for themselves. Unless they are operating in Era 3 as well, it is very likely they will not be able to match the mutual understanding that you have achieved with customers. Your competitors are in a no-win position: you represent clarity and credibility, and they represent uncertainty. Now, the only task left in the Design phase is confirmation.

Avoiding the Three Traps of the Design Phase

There are three common traps that salespeople need to recognize and avoid in defining solution expectations:

PREMATURE PRESENTATION

When customers begin talking about expectations, there is always a temptation, often an irresistible one, for the salesperson to slip into presentation. Customers say they expect high reliability as a solution outcome, and suddenly the salesperson is delivering a speech about the consistent and reliable performance of the offering. We need to be aware of this and avoid the urge to present during the Design phase.

UNPAID CONSULTING

Unpaid consulting starts when we cross the line between defining *parameters* of a solution and designing solutions. When we start *designing solutions*, we are acting as consultants. In past decades, this was not a monumental issue. If you figured out the problem and designed a unique and competent solution for a customer, the sale was almost guaranteed and you were rewarded for your consulting effort.

Today, however, there is an ever-increasing proliferation of competitors, and once a solution is designed, the customer can easily shop it to the competition. When that happens, we become unpaid consultants and our own worst enemies. We've enabled our competitor, who did not make the investment in the diagnosis or in designing the actual solution, to sell its solution at a lower price. We can avoid this trap in one of two ways: either by staying focused on the customer's expectations for solution outcomes and not straying into the design of solutions, or by charging customers for our design services.

CREEPING ELEGANCE

The final pitfall occurs when customers become so enthusiastic about the potential value of solutions to their problems that they expand the scope of the outcomes. When customers drop into this "as long as we're going to do this, we might as well also do that" mode of thinking, they tend to lose their sense of fiscal responsibility, and conventional salespeople start to count the extra commissions coming their way.

The problem with allowing creeping elegance lies in the very nature of the complex sale. There is no single decision maker in the sale, so if you allow one member of the cast of characters to unnecessarily expand the scope of a solution, you are risking the entire project because it is highly probable that it will be sniped at by other members of the cast and could be shot down.

Instead, you must ensure that the solution does not expand beyond reasonable financial parameters and help customers determine any additional costs or risks they could incur if it does. The rule to follow is this: never allow an expectation that is not backed up by a specific problem and a cost that supports the additional investment.

Confirmation and the Discussion Document

In the Prime Process, confirmation is driven by a *discussion document*. Discussion documents are much like sketches that architects draw. In designing a building, an architect and the client first discuss the features that the client wants in the design; the architect then draws a preliminary sketch based on those requirements. Next, a process of iteration ensues as the client and the architect refine and enhance the design and the sketches become more and more complete. You can't actually construct a building from these drawings, but they do serve as a starting point for the blueprints.

The discussion document is very similar to the architect's sketch. Sales professionals are creating this living document throughout the Prime Process. Think of it as a tool to clarify critical communications during the decision process. It should start as early as the first conversation and serve as a recap of that discussion. You could send the document to your customer, requesting that he or she review your notes and make any required revisions. The discussion document should continue to grow and be revised as the decision process proceeds.

By the Design phase, the discussion document should contain all of the information that has been obtained during the Discover and Diagnose phases. Now that the solution parameters have been determined, they should be added to the discussion document and a final draft should be prepared. This final draft recaps the overall situation, its financial impact, the customer's expectations, and the solution parameters on which the best solution will be determined. It sums up the entire sales engagement to this point and puts into writing the findings, agreements, and understandings reached with the customer.

When a customer does not agree with an item in the discussion document, you know that an impediment to a successful sale has surfaced. Before you can move forward with the engagement, you need to trace each concern or disconnect back to its source and resolve it to the customer's satisfaction.

Conversely, when the customer does confirm the contents of the discussion document, it tells you two things: First, all of the requirements needed to create and deliver the best solution have been addressed. Second, it is now the right time to formally offer the customer that solution. It is time to move into the final phase of the Prime Process: Deliver.

Key Thought
What's Wrong with This Picture?

Salespeople tend to forget that there are always conflicting objectives coexisting within organizations. When the design of a solution that is clearly in the best interest of the organization is meeting resistance, you must first ask yourself, "What is wrong with this picture?" When you identify what it is that doesn't make sense, ask a second question, "Under what circumstances would this refusal to confirm make sense?"

Normally, the answers to these two questions lead you to one or more members of the cast of characters who believe that they will experience pain because of the solution. You can neutralize that pain by recognizing it and addressing it in the solution, or by building a consensus that it must be accepted for the overall benefit of the organization.

Deliver the Value

Creating Competitor-Proof Customer Relationships

We frequently hear similar statements from executives when they call on us to help them improve their organization's sales and marketing performance. They express concerns like: "We have the right solution and our team does a great job of communicating our value, but we struggle in the final phases of the sale. We're good at selling customers our value, but then we get beat up on price. We just can't hold our ground during the close and negotiations."

You no doubt recognize what's right and what's wrong with these statements. The statement of the problem—getting "beat up on price," which is likely causing declining sales and profit margins—is based on fact and represents a very real and serious situation. However, the identification of the causes of the problem—the inability of salespeople to close and negotiate—is an opinion and, in reality, neither is an actual cause of the problem.

Closing and negotiation skills in the conventional sense are rarely needed in the properly executed diagnostic sales engagement. More accurately, you don't need to worry about closing and negotiation during the eleventh hour if you follow the Prime Process. These two most onerous and often feared tasks in sales are simply no longer necessary.

This is a difficult idea for salespeople to grasp. "What? No objections? No negotiations?" Their incredulity is a measure of how deeply the conventional selling mind-set is still ingrained in the psyche of the salespeople and how radical a shift away from that mind-set the Prime Process continues to represent.

The Prime Process nullifies the dependency on closing and negotiation skills because by the time the decision process reaches the Deliver phase, your customers will have already passed through the Diagnose and Design phases. In Diagnose, they have understood and confirmed the risks they are facing and their causes, along with the resulting consequences and their financial impact. They will have determined that it is now a priority and they must make changes to their current situation. In Design, they have explored and decided on their expected outcomes, the best solution approach to assure success, the expected investment and financial return, the implementation time schedule, and finally, the selection criteria. They have defined all of the parameters of a high-quality solution. Now, in the Deliver phase, as long as your offerings address these pre-established elements, all of your customer's concerns have been met. There is literally nothing for them to object to and no reason to question the price of your products and services. If any unexpected questions do surface, they can simply be linked back to the information that you've already developed and confirmed with them.

Negotiation takes on a new definition in the Diagnostic Business Development approach. The essence of the approach is clear and precise communication and collaboration, leading to a continuous state of mutual understanding. The process of creating such a state is negotiation at its most evolved level. This open collaboration from moment one ensures that the sale proceeds by mutual agreement through each decision milestone.

If sales professionals are still engaged with their customers by the time the Deliver phase is reached, they have successfully provided their customers with the confidence to invest in their solutions and passed all the decision tests required to win the sale. This translates to no objections, no price negotiations and pressure, and no buyer's remorse and other deal-canceling reactions. It also means shorter sales cycles, more predictable outcomes, and higher margin transactions—all of the things that define individual and business success in sales.

So, what should we be doing at the conclusion of the Prime Process? The final phase of the process, Deliver, is focused on two goals: (1) the confirmation of the customer's decision and the completion of the sale, and (2) the successful achievement of the solution's value and the establishment of a competitor-proof post-sale relationship among the salesperson, his or her company, and the customer.

Elements of the first goal, successful completion, include formalizing the sale and then delivering and implementing the solution. The sale is formalized when the salesperson prepares and presents the proposal and the customer accepts it. In delivery and implementation of solutions, sales professionals work with colleagues in their own and their customers' companies to manage the change process required to use the solution, mitigate the risks in the implementation, and ensure that their customers are achieving and measuring the value they have been promised.

The second goal of the Deliver phase is focused on value achievement and post-sale relationship building. It includes (1) monitoring, adjustment (if necessary), and communication of solution outcomes; and (2) the expansion of the business relationship that the sales professional has been building throughout the Prime Process. We call individuals who successfully establish this expanded role Prime Resources®, because they are true business advisors and have become the preferred providers for their products and services in their customers' minds. They are seen as a source of business advantage to their customers and their own company.

Key Thought
If You Were Your Customer, Would You Do What You Are
About to Recommend?

Before you enter the Deliver phase, there is one question to ask yourself: If you were the customer, knowing what you know, would you do what you are about to recommend? This is the ultimate integrity test—a primary tenet of ethical selling and the basis for long-term relationships. Imagine that the customer is your best friend or that you are the doctor and the customer is your patient. Would you be offering the same solution? If not, now is the time to stop the process, take a step back, and reconsider the alternatives.

Formalizing the Sale

The first thing that we deliver in the final phase of the Prime Process is the proposal. The proposal is a formal, polished version of the final draft of the discussion document that we reviewed at the end of the Design phase. It is the complete story of the best solution for the customer, as it describes what that solution is and how we arrived at it.

The proposal lays out all of the technical specifications of the solution and the contractual details that go into a binding agreement. Like the discussion document, the proposal summarizes all the findings you have developed thus far and the decisions that the customer has made. It is an extension of the discussion document, and it leads the customer step-by-step, back over the *Bridge to Change*, from the solution itself to the decision criteria and outcome expectations, to the problem indicators and consequences, and on to the customer's performance objectives. This articulation and summary of the chain of decisions also takes into consideration and addresses the critical perspectives of each member of the cast of characters. It reinforces his or her *incentive to change* and *confidence to invest*.

The proposal in the Prime Process is an instrument of confirmation. It is a formal statement of everything that has already been agreed on. It should contain no new information; it should inspire no debate. It is only the formal conclusion of a sale that has already been agreed on.

Key Thought
No Surprises

Lawyers are taught never to ask a witness a question unless they already know how the witness will answer. The same advice holds true for proposals in complex sales: Never put anything in a proposal that the customer has not already agreed to and confirmed. When we surprise our customers with new information in proposals, they will surely surprise us with unexpected, and usually negative, responses.

When we use the word "confirmation" to describe a proposal in the Prime Process, we are making an important distinction between it and the typical sales proposal. In conventional sales, the proposal is used as an instrument of *consideration*. In other words, it is presented to customers so that they can analyze and judge the solution being proposed. That is why the content of most sales proposals is devoted almost exclusively (usually 80 percent or more) to the solution being offered. It is also why most proposals go through multiple revisions and lead to protracted sales cycles.

The problem is that proposals devoted to solutions do not tell the full story of the engagement. (Often, there is no story to tell because the sales engagement has not been properly completed.) They don't explain the customer's situation, the evidence of risk, the quantification of value, or how the solution being proposed is connected to the customer's business objectives. As a result, proposals are incomplete, unconvincing, and serve mainly to provoke objections. The conventional solution-focused proposal is full of pitfalls.

Further, as discussed earlier, proposals focused on the salesperson's offering are largely a waste of time. They all sound alike to customers, who invariably find it difficult to connect the solution's features and benefits to their performance metrics, and to quantify the true value of the solution. Therefore, proposals unerringly lead customers to decisions that deteriorate to the lowest common denominator—*price*. (They also inhibit the salesperson's ability to differentiate his or her company and offerings, another example of self-commoditization.)

A few recommendations specifically for practitioners of the Prime Process follow.

Write for the Invisible Decision Maker

Recently, I analyzed a proposal prepared by an outsourcing company in the commercial insurance industry. The company was offering to take over control of the management of all of a client's insurance needs. The client represented a large account, almost ten times the size of the company's average customer. The service being offered was complex; the proposal, on the other hand, was two pages long. The first page specified the rates per $100 in salary by the job classifications of the client's employees. The second page specified a rebate that would be earned if the client's incurred loss ratio remained below certain levels. That was the entire proposal. Picture yourself as a senior executive with the prospective client who wasn't involved in the engagement to this point, but is being asked to approve this sale. Would you green light this expenditure? On what grounds?

Proposals need to be written for the invisible decision maker, not because there always is one, but because proposals need to tell the entire story of the engagement—and the decisions that have been made during it—convincingly and coherently. That typically means that less than 30 percent of the proposal should be about your solution—the vast majority of it should be about the customer's situation, objectives, and the solution parameters required to achieve success. When we keep the imaginary reader in our minds as we prepare the proposal, we have a constant sounding board for the content. It can guide us to a proposal that is a business report—one that explains a problem, the parameters of a solution, and the solution itself.

Echo the Customer's Voice

When we speak with clients who are interested in our services, we record the calls and conversations whenever possible and take copious notes when we can't record them. There is no ulterior motive here; what we are doing is trying to capture the voice of the customer.

All organizations have their own language. There are special phrases and meanings that make sense to and strike chords in the people who work within them. Listen for key phrases and adopt them. Echo this language in your proposal and your customers will hear themselves speaking and reinforce their decision to take action. Customers should not be able to distinguish the proposal from an internal report prepared by someone in their own company.

Enlist the Cast of Characters

The cast of characters is the salesperson's primary source of information throughout the Prime Process. When the time comes to review the proposal, we can enlist their help once more by asking members of the cast to present selected portions of the proposal themselves.

We can arrange this ahead of the meeting and call on these cast members during the presentation, saying, for example, "Bill, this information on page 10 grew out of our discussions. Maybe you want to walk us through it." Hearing a colleague present sends a powerful message of support for the proposal and confirmation for the solution to the rest of the decision team.

Go for the No One More Time

When our customers indicate their acceptance of the proposal, it is time to *go for the no* once more. Throughout the Prime Process, we have indicated our readiness to walk away from the engagement any time that the customer decides that there is no good reason to continue.

What would you say to a friend who has told you that he has made a major decision? You would probably ask, "Are you sure?" We establish ourselves as "best friend" and valued business advisor one more time when we ask customers questions such as, "Are we still on the right track? Are there additional questions that we haven't covered? Has anything changed since we finalized the document? Did we miss anything?" Further, if the customer is not sure about the decision, we find out on the spot (not three days later) and have the opportunity to resolve any doubts that still exist.

Delivering the Solution

What does the conventional salesperson do after the sale is closed? Move on to the next victim. That sounds harsh, but unfortunately, that is exactly how many customers believe salespeople behave. The most successful salespeople deal with this prejudice by breaking type once again and remaining conspicuously involved in the delivery and implementation of solutions.

Your involvement in the delivery of the solution grows out of a simple idea: *an order does not make a relationship.* Relationships are built on dependability, trust, and the customer's ability and willingness to rely on your expertise whenever he or she needs assistance. When salespeople hand off customers and move on to new customers, no matter how smooth and problem-free the process, customers are going to perceive this as an abandonment of the relationship. It also leaves them wondering how well they will be supported in the future.

We are not saying that salespeople should spend all of their time delivering solutions and working with existing customers. Obviously, a major part of a salesperson's job is to discover, engage, and establish new accounts. Too often, however, salespeople move on too quickly. We need to recognize the value of existing customers and devote a significant portion of our time to the retention and expansion of our relationships with those customers. This value is well documented. For example, a classic study by Bain & Company calculated that a 5 percent increase in retention could result in profit increases ranging from 25 percent to 100 percent.[1] When salespeople stay directly involved with customers during and after the delivery of the solution, they capture a sizable opportunity.

The Implementation Satisfaction Curve

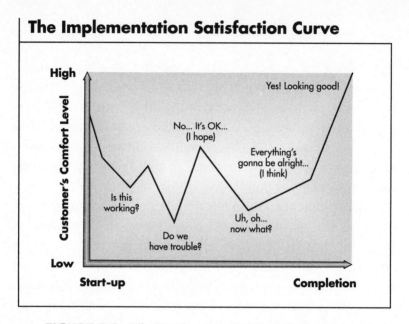

FIGURE 7.1   The Implementation Satisfaction Curve

The same cooperative and diagnostic skills that carried us through the previous phases of the Prime Process are put to work in the physical delivery of the solution. The best sales professionals start this work by confronting and communicating the implementation challenges that their customers regularly encounter. If your company never has implementation problems, this doesn't apply. However, in our experience, that is rarely the case. We find that the typical solution implementation and a customer's reaction to it look something like Figure 7.1.

Typically, salespeople gloss over discussions regarding the ups and downs of implementation. Perhaps, hoping that problems will not occur, they try to ignore them. Thus, when problems do pop up, customers are not anticipating them and are caught by surprise, maximizing their dissatisfaction. This, in turn, forces the salesperson and the service and support staff to spend too much time in damage control and recovery, or risk a worse reaction from the unhappy customer.

One way in which this negative cycle can be avoided is by analyzing the problems and negative reactions that tend to surface in delivery, and defusing them before their occurrence. Defusing potential problems before they occur is an excellent, practical solution to delivery snafus, but we also recognize that salespeople won't be able to anticipate every implementation problem. Another way to break the negative cycle that begins when customers are unpleasantly surprised during implementation is to adopt a mind-set that admits the possibility of problems and prepares you to address them.

I'm reminded of the time when a good friend was facing the prospect of a triple bypass surgery and a heart valve replacement. I was with his family when the surgeon came in to brief him and answer his questions. They told me how the surgeon described the surgery and said, "I want to caution you, when you wake up in the recovery room, you will question whether you are alive. You will be restrained with straps and unable to move. You won't be able to talk due to the respirator tube in your throat. The effects of the drugs will make your thinking clouded and you will feel like a truck has driven over your chest a couple of times." It struck me that this little "pep talk" was a bit over the top, but then I thought about the alternative. What if the surgeon had said nothing and my friend woke up and experienced all those things without realizing they were normal? He would certainly be anxious and might panic. As difficult as it would be to cope with the surgery, his reactions could make it much worse. He also may have been very bitter that he hadn't been warned.

The fact that customers experience problems in the implementation of a solution is often less of an issue than how salespeople react when problems do occur. The best sales professionals prepare for these problems by admitting that they exist, providing the customer with the means to report them, and, most importantly, by reacting to reported problems in a cooperative manner, thereby acting as a business partner and diagnostician.

Key Thought
You Must *Be Prepared to Not Be Prepared.*

Like pilots who are trained to react to emergencies almost reflexively and without panic, sales professionals also need to *be prepared to not be prepared.* They must be so prepared that their response seems natural and spontaneous. They remain cool, calm, and collected when confronted by upset customers. They say, "That is not good to hear. I'm sorry this has happened to you." They then move immediately into diagnosis, "When you say it doesn't work, help me understand. Walk me through it."

Measuring and Reporting Results—Value Achieved

After the solution has been delivered and implemented, the sales professional has one final task. The last step in the Deliver phase and the end of the Diagnostic process itself is the measurement and reporting of the results generated by the solution.

Of all the sales methodologies, the Prime Process best equips sales professionals to measure and report results. We already worked with our customers to determine and agree on the indicators of the problem, its financial impact, and expectations of the solution and its value. In Deliver, we simply turn back to these metrics, measure them against the actual results, and report our findings to the customer at various stages during implementation and use of the solution.

If the expected outcomes have not been achieved, we prove our value and professionalism to the customer once again by diagnosing the obstacles that are holding them back and then designing new solutions. If the expected outcomes are being achieved, it is critical to document the results and leverage them to open new business opportunities with the customer.

Salespeople should undertake the work of measuring and reporting customer results for the following three compelling reasons:

1. It ensures that the promised outcomes and associated value have been achieved. We may be able to succeed in the short term by closing sales and moving on to new customers, but to succeed over the long term, we must deliver on our promises.

2. It provides the basis for re-engaging in the Prime Process. I call my sales methodology a process, but it is also a cycle. When our customers achieve or exceed the outcomes they envisioned for the solution, we can continue the Prime Process by using their results to move back into the diagnostic mode, uncovering new risks that can undermine their success or new opportunities that can enhance it. Then we can design new solutions that are capable of providing improved results.

3. It allows us to establish our position as one of our customer's preferred resources, which maximizes the long-term profitability of the customer relationship and erects impenetrable barriers to our competitors.

The ultimate goal is to become business advisors and our customer's Prime Resource for the solutions we bring to market. In the customer's mind, this relationship sets us apart from the competition and positions us in an ongoing role as a source of business advantage and a contributor to the customer's success.

The following are five characteristics of a Prime Resource:

1. A Prime Resource is an active participant in his or her customers' businesses. These sales professionals understand their customers' business requirements and performance measurements and take an active role in their success.

2. A Prime Resource is committed to long-term growth relationships with customers. These sales professionals allocate the time and energy required to work with customers on a regular basis.

3. A Prime Resource bases recommendations on measurable problems and outcomes. These sales professionals are always working from the reality of the customer's world.

4. A Prime Resource acts as an early warning system for customers. These sales professionals uncover unexposed problems and notify customers of changes in products, technologies, and markets that may impact their businesses.

5. A Prime Resource stays close. These sales professionals know that two-thirds of customers stop doing business with companies because they feel unappreciated, neglected, or treated indifferently.[2]

If it sounds as though there is a good deal of work involved in becoming a Prime Resource, there is. At least, there is more work than the conventional salesperson typically dedicates to their customers' success, but the rewards are exponentially higher.

In the "you snooze, you lose" world of business, a Prime Resource is always awake and alert to significant changes in the environment. His or her customers learn to depend on this alertness and become loyal, long-term customers.

Further, your best customer is always your competitor's best prospect. The customers of a Prime professional, however, have a much higher resistance level than the average customer. Customers know the value that they derive from a Prime relationship. So when competitors call and say, "We can give you the same thing for 10 to 20 percent less," Prime customers don't get lured away. They know the right questions to ask and the traps to avoid. They are also well aware of all of the decisions that go into choosing a high-quality solution—after all, that is exactly what you have taught them in the Prime Process.

Driving Predictable and Profitable Organic Growth: Building a Diagnostic Business Development Capability

Building a Value-Driven
Sales Organization

Getting Paid for the Value You Create

Diagnostic Business Development is the best way to align the sales organization with the conditions and customer demands of Era 3. In Parts One and Two of this book, I described how its systems, skills, and disciplines can become a springboard to success for individual sales professionals. Now I'd like to address how sales leaders can leverage Diagnostic Business Development into a *functional capability* that can improve performance across the sales organization.

Sales executives and managers are charged with producing superlative sales results on a consistent basis in every kind of economic environment. They are expected to accurately forecast sales revenue and create organic growth by meeting the sales targets that these forecasts yield. They are responsible for managing and maintaining the primary interface between their companies and their customers. They have very challenging and high-pressure jobs.

Sales leaders can only achieve these tasks through their sales organization. Sales organizations have a lot in common with professional sports teams. Many of them have enjoyed short-term runs of success. Maybe a dream team comes together or the competition falls apart or perhaps the planets line up just right for a season or two. However, teams that win over the long term—in professional sports and sales—are much less common.

When you examine sports teams that win consistently from season to season, you often find legendary leaders—individuals such as Vince Lombardi and Don Shula in football, Phil Jackson in basketball, and Roger Penske and Ross Brawn in auto racing. These leaders don't rely on luck.

As Joe Gibbs, the first person to ever lead championship teams in both professional football and NASCAR auto racing, explains, "A win at any track doesn't just happen by accident. We don't simply fill our cars with gas, crank them up, and hope we can drive faster or outlast our opponents. Every detail of the race is thought through, including contingency plans and backup parts. We have a game plan for the race and we attempt to follow it as closely as possible."[1] In other words, sports teams that win consistently have an effective strategy and they execute it as flawlessly as possible. Their leaders build sports dynasties by adopting and implementing such systems, managing and refining them, and recruiting, training, and coaching players who are capable of executing them with exceptional discipline day in and day out. They literally institutionalize the ability to win, raising it to the level of a capability. The best sales leaders seek to achieve exactly the same thing.

Beyond the Black Box

The sales function has always been something of a black box on the organizational chart. The fact that so many organizations accept such a wide range of performance in a major function suggests that what goes on within the black box continues to be a great mystery. No company would tolerate such performance variation in a manufacturing line.

There are several reasons why the sales function is so poorly understood. First, although the sales organization is the primary generator of revenue in most companies, it is too often treated as a non-value-added "distributor" of goods and services. This view harkens back to a less competitive, less complex business era, when companies produced goods and services, and salespeople simply presented them to customers who were happy to get them. Even the great management thinker Peter Drucker felt confident enough to declare that sales was a "superfluous" function.

He said that the aim of marketing was to "know and understand the customer so well that the product or service fits him and sells itself." He only grudgingly admitted, "There will always, one can assume, be need for some selling."[2] Obviously, Drucker did not foresee the rise in complexity in business-to-business markets and the guidance that customers would require to achieve value.

Second, sales has not been considered a professional discipline. Although the tide has turned in recent years and sales degrees are becoming more common, sales was never a well-established part of the business curriculum in colleges and universities. Because sales has not been a prominent subject among academics, it hasn't been researched in the same depth as other business disciplines, such as management, operations, and marketing. Accordingly, it does not have a deep, established body of knowledge, and the senior leaders of companies tend to understand sales only to the degree that they have had direct experience in the function or have been on the receiving end of a sales pitch (which typically doesn't exemplify the profession at its best).

Third, the sales function is executed "out there." Because the sales organization can be widely dispersed and spends much of its time in the field, the function tends to be physically separated from the rest of the organization and the attention of senior leadership. Attention is paid to sales forecasts and results, but what happens in between is generally taken for granted until results don't live up to expectations. Then, since no one knows exactly what went wrong, there tends to be a lot of finger-pointing, changes in leadership, and ad hoc training and motivation—none of which produce permanent change or significant results.

The best sales leaders reject the traditional view of their function (see Figure 8.1). They strive to make the sales function transparent and accountable, and to enhance sales results and predictability. If they aren't generating the

The Top Five Excuses for Sales as Usual

"We only hire experienced professionals."
Translation: we don't have a system for developing successful salespeople.

"The sales force is made of creative and independent individuals."
Translation: we can't control them.

"It takes six to nine months to learn our business."
Translation: it will be at least a year before we can judge their productivity.

"They've got some good irons in the fire."
Translation: there's lots of smoke, but we have no idea how the sales engagements are progressing.

"You just can't find good people anymore."
Translation: we don't know where to look or what to look for.

FIGURE 8.1   The Top Five Excuses for Sales as Usual

performance results they need, they don't simply step on the gas, trying to prod the sales organization into doing more of what isn't working in the first place. They know that if they do, they will be forced to depend almost exclusively on the innate talents of individual salespeople. Given the fact that only 3 to 6 percent of salespeople are able to figure out how to sell effectively in Era 3 on their own, this virtually guarantees mediocre results.

Instead, the most successful sales leaders try to help their teams to work smarter instead of harder. They recognize that how their sales forces engage customers has a far greater impact on their results than how many customers they engage. In response, they strive to create a sales capability that supports accountability, predictability, and exceptional performance.

In management terms, a capability is the capacity of an organization to do something that gives it an advantage in the marketplace. Individual employees exercise a capability, but the capability resides in the organization. A capability doesn't disappear when one or more employees leave the organization. If it does disappear when employees leave, it was an ability that only one or more individuals shared, as opposed to an organizational capability.

Often capabilities are defined in functional terms:

- Toyota developed a manufacturing capability that enabled it to produce high-quality, low-cost cars and eventually became the world's largest automaker by sales.
- Nike developed a design capability that enabled it to create footwear and apparel that came to define the state of the art in athletes' minds.
- Cisco developed a capability for mergers and acquisitions that enabled it to attain and maintain a leadership position in an industry defined by fast-paced technological change.
- Similarly, a sales department can develop a capability for Diagnostic Business Development that creates a competitive advantage and drives profitable organic growth. It is a capability in which the sales organization itself is a key differentiator in the marketplace. As you have already read, this capability is based on clarifying and achieving customer value—a prerequisite for succeeding in the complex business-to-business markets of Era 3.

Creating a Diagnostic Business Development Capability in Sales

To create a Diagnostic Business Development capability within the sales function, we need to embed its systems, skills, and discipline into the DNA of the sales organization.

This requires an integrated and sustained effort that is foreign to many sales leaders.

In sales, performance improvement is generally pursued at one of two levels: the *event* level or the *process* level.

The event level, which I sometimes call the "inoculation approach" because of its ad hoc, one-shot nature, is the most common approach to performance improvement. Are sales results lagging? It's time to call a company-wide sales meeting, bring in the most popular speaker we can afford, and give everyone a motivational jolt. Having trouble getting appointments or converting proposals to sales? Let's run an online training seminar on cold calling or give every salesperson a book that promises to reveal the secrets to closing sales. At best, events like these encourage salespeople to "grab one or two ideas" and use them to improve their performance. This can create a short-term bump in results, but performance virtually always returns to the norm because there is a lack of support and reinforcement. At worst, event-based improvement efforts often detract from performance by taking up valuable time that salespeople could be spending in the field and teaching tactics that will likely fail without the proper mind-set and context for their use.

At the process level, sales leaders acknowledge that the way the sales organization is selling isn't working and they try to address the issue by turning their attention from improving salespeople to improving the process they are using. Their intent is sound. Experts such as W. Edwards Deming taught us long ago that fixing a process has a much greater impact on output than trying to fix the people who execute it. The problem in seeking performance improvement at the process level is that it is not enough. Sales leaders tend to alter their company's sales process or adopt an entirely new process without fully considering what other elements must be in place to implement, support, and use it. Far too often, they neglect the cultural and skill demands of the new process. As a result, the sales organization rejects the change or destroys its effectiveness by force fitting it into the organization's established selling methods and practices. When this happens, sales results can actually get worse.

In the past few years, one of the more common process-level initiatives that I have seen companies undertake in sales has been Six Sigma. The intent of Six Sigma is certainly valid—it seeks improved results by continuously refining a process. It is a great idea *if* you are already using an effective process. But what happens when you seek to refine a process that is fundamentally flawed? If you are working with an Era 1 or Era 2 process, Six Sigma enables your salespeople to work ineffectively more efficiently. It magnifies the flaws in your sales process, producing temporary, incremental gains by doing more of what you are doing, but missing the breakthrough gains that are possible when you successfully engineer an innovative and more effective process.

You can't create a capability within a sales organization by working only at the event or process levels. Embedding a capability in a function—institutionalizing it, so to speak—requires a higher-level approach, a *transformative* performance improvement effort that is conducted in an integrated and sustainable fashion. As Shumeet Banerji, Paul Leinwand, and Cesare Mainardi of Booz & Company wrote, "Capabilities are the interconnected people, knowledge, systems, tools, and processes that establish a company's right to win in a given industry or business."[3]

To create a Diagnostic Business Development capability, the leaders of the sales function must provide the entire sales organization with all three essential elements that I defined in Chapter 3: a system, which is the process that will guide the sales organization through the sales cycle; skills, which will help the sales organization execute the process; and discipline, which will give the sales organization the emotional strength or stamina needed to adopt a new mind-set and stick with it. Leave out one or more of these elements and the capability can't take root or grow properly.

Executive Ownership

A new capability is built from the bottom up, but it will not take hold and flourish without support from the top down. The company's senior sales executive is the most likely keeper of the functional capability. This means that he or she will act as a sponsor who understands the connection between the new sales capability and the success of the company in its marketplace, serves as an internal advocate for the capability throughout the organization, and plays a direct, hands-on role in supervising development of the capability.

When my colleagues and I work with companies to build a Diagnostic Business Development capability within the sales organization, we ensure that all three elements are properly integrated and adopted by following a three-stage implementation framework:

- First, we help the sales leaders clarify the value of their solutions and create a tailored Diagnostic Business Development platform that will enable the sales organization to connect and quantify that value with customers.

- Second, we work with them to validate the new platform by testing it in the field, achieving early wins, and documenting its success.

- Third, we assist them in transforming the platform into a capability by implementing it across the sales organization and preparing the sales organization to use it.

Stage 1: Developing a Tailored Platform

Diagnostic Business Development is a value-based platform and capability. Therefore, the sales leadership team must develop a comprehensive understanding of the quantitative and qualitative value that a company's solutions provide to customers and then, based on that value, design a tailored platform—which encompasses the system, skills, and discipline—for Diagnostic Business Development.

The initial value clarity analysis must be conducted from the customer's perspective. It must also be very precise and linked to real conditions in the company's customer segments. This is especially important because customers throughout the business-to-business sector are suffering from ROI and value fatigue: they have been bombarded with generic value propositions and ROI calculators to the point that they no longer consider it credible when salespeople talk about ROI and value.

To clarify the value of solutions, we enlist the help of a small set of leaders who are familiar with various aspects of the complete value picture. They understand how the solution is designed to create value and they understand how value is actually achieved within the customer's business. These leaders are usually drawn from several functions within the company, such as R&D, engineering, manufacturing, marketing, and service. We ask this team to describe the value that their solutions are capable of delivering and how that value manifests in the customer's world. We challenge their thinking, clarify their value descriptions, and identify points of value differentiation by asking questions such as, "How do you know that's what one of your customers would say?" and "Could your competitor honestly make the same claim?"

The goal of this exercise is twofold. First, we are seeking to ensure that all of the value of the solutions is accounted for. (As I will explain in greater detail in Chapter 9, a substantial amount of value "leaks" out of solutions on their journeys to customers.) Second, every facet of value must be connected to the customer segment's business performance metrics, and the financial impact of the absence of that lack of value on the segment's bottom line must be quantified. Once value is properly and fully clarified, the leadership team can focus its attention on defining and designing the system, skills, and discipline of the platform.

"We've Already Done That!"

When describing the value clarity analysis to sales executives, they sometimes say something like, "We've already done that. We worked with marketing to develop a value proposition and we know exactly what and how much value we bring to the table." Here is a very simple self-assessment based on seven questions to help you test the reality of that statement:

1. Have you been able to clarify all the value your solution provides to your customers?

2. Have you been able to connect that value to the various business drivers and performance metrics within your customer's organization?

3. Have you been able to isolate the performance impacts to specific jobs that are responsible for those metrics?

4. Have you been able to help the customer co-author a dollar amount to the impact your value has with a number that the customer agrees with?

5. Have you been able to identify all the constraints that your customers face in trying to optimize the value they can receive from your solution?

6. Have you provided your customer with the ability to address those constraints and manage the changes they need to make?

7. Are you able to measure the value you have delivered and has your customer agreed with the amount you have measured?

If you can't answer each question with a whole-hearted "yes," it is highly likely that a cross-functional value clarity analysis would be a worthy investment of executive time and effort.

Designing the System: Although specific deliverables will vary with each sales organization, the core system of the Diagnostic Business Development platform will always follow the same pattern as the Prime Process. It must include the Discover, Diagnose, Design, and Deliver phases and in each phase, guide the customer through key decisions and produce the outcomes needed to move the customer to the next higher stage of the Value Life Cycle in the pursuit of value achievement.

The degree of effort required to design such a system will vary by how well-suited your current sales process is to the dynamics of Era 3. Some companies, especially those that depend on individual salespeople to provide the process or are still using a sales process better suited to Era 1, may need to start their design from a clean slate. Others, such as those who are using Era 2 processes like solution selling, may be able to redesign certain phases and/or fill gaps in their existing process.

A good way to gauge the design effort that will be needed in your company is to consider how long your sales process has been in place and the last time that its basic steps were modified. Ask yourself whether the process is primarily focused on the activities and outcomes of the salesperson or the customer. Describe the stages of your process. If you find yourself using words such as "demonstrate," "present," "negotiate," "prove," and "close" (instead of words such as "evidence," "financial impact," "criteria," and "consensus"), it is likely that the focus of the process is misplaced. Sales executives are often surprised to realize that they are asking their salespeople to be customer-focused, but are providing them with a process that hardly considers the customer.

The system design team must also consider how the tailored Prime Process will be integrated and aligned with existing systems and processes within the sales function. In most cases, this will require changes that will improve the outcomes of these systems and processes. For example, what is the basis for your current forecasts? Usually, they are based on the best guesses of individual salespeople as to how "interested" their customers are and how soon they might sign a deal. If you change the forecasting process and align it to a tailored Prime Process, you can greatly improve the accuracy of your forecasts and enhance accountability. The Prime Process allows you to create a common language and specific milestones for determining where customers are in the sales cycle. Forecasting, like the sales process, becomes driven by evidence gathered from customers versus an opinion on the part of a salesperson.

Developing the Skills and Creating the Tools: With the design for a tailored Prime Process in hand, the leadership team can turn its attention to skills that salespeople will need to execute the process and the tools that will support those skills. Thinking back to Chapter 3, the foundational skills of Diagnostic Business Development are the ability of salespeople to identify the right people within the customer's company and ask them the right questions in the right sequence. In stage 1 of developing a Diagnostic Business Development capability, the design team needs to consider how the sales organization will learn how to do this, and it needs to create the tools that will support these tasks.

The "right people" component of the skills equation requires that the team equip the sales organization to identify the cast of characters in a typical sale. This requires that the team think beyond job titles, which can often be deceiving, and create a list of the responsibilities of the victims (those people within customer companies who are typically affected by the lack of the value being sold).

Next, the team needs to begin constructing diagnostic conversational maps—similar to the decision trees that doctors use to determine the health of the patient and diagnose diseases and other health issues—for each member of the cast of characters that cover the customer's entire decision process. Questioning and listening skills have been taught to salespeople for decades, and they've been equipped with long lists of generic questions. Now we need to take an evolutionary leap and begin teaching and equipping them to have higher-level conversations. This is how we ensure that the "right questions" are asked in the "right sequence."

The design team must create a number of other tools, especially the measurement tools that salespeople need if they are to quantify value. These include tools to quantify the cost of the problem, the value of the solution, and appropriate investment in the solution (as described in Chapters 5 and 6).

The design team must also consider how salespeople will learn the skills necessary to navigate the Prime Process and utilize these tools. This will almost certainly require

Sales Training Self-Assessment

In complex sales, we can divide optimal sales education into three categories: (1) Product Knowledge, the study of the features and benefits of the products and services you offer and how they impact the business drivers of the customer; (2) Diagnostics, the study of the customer's business, job responsibilities, and the skills needed to uncover problems the customer is experiencing; and (3) Solutions, the study of how to solve customer problems and how our products and services relate to those problems.

How does your current sales training relate to these categories?

What percentage of your training falls into each?

Product Knowledge   _____ %

Diagnostics   _____ %

Solutions   _____ %

FIGURE 8.2 Sales Training Self-Assessment

that the team consider and modify the current sales development curriculum. In my experience, the content of sales training is overwhelmingly focused on solutions. Even though salespeople are constantly told to understand the customer before they present, solution training simply does not equip them to do this (see Figure 8.2). Instead, we should be designing training that focuses on critical business issues, job responsibilities, indicators, causes, consequences, and expectations within our customers' companies, and only then, connecting those realities back to the specific value creation capabilities of our solutions.

Instilling the Discipline: The final element of the Diagnostic Business Development platform that the design team must consider is the most challenging. The challenge arises because instilling a discipline in a sales organization requires that everyone who works with and within it changes how they think about selling. We are talking about changes in the culture of the sales organization, an inherently challenging, yet rewarding process.

As the design team approaches the discipline challenge, its members should first consider the role model that the sales organization should adopt. I would point to a combination of doctor, detective, and best friend described in Chapter 3. We want a sales organization composed of cool, calm, and collected diagnostic professionals who are well-prepared and able to execute a well-defined system using finely honed skills. Think of Captain Chesley "Sully" Sullenberger, the US Air pilot, who, within 90 seconds of takeoff had to react quickly and flawlessly to safely land a stalled Airbus A320 full of people. "We had lost both engines at a low speed, at a low altitude, over one of the most densely populated areas of the planet," he said in an interview on CBS's *60 Minutes*. "I knew it was a very challenging situation."[4]

With a role model in mind, the team needs to think ahead to how the new mind-set will be instilled and reinforced in the sales organization. Certainly a development effort will be required, but more important than that, a great deal of modeling, mentoring, and coaching by senior and line sales managers will be a critical factor in assisting salespeople as they establish and maintain their new mind-set. Unfortunately, such dictates of time almost always become a barrier in the creation of cultural change. To overcome this constraint, the design team needs to consider whether sales managers have the required level of coaching skills and the time they will need to serve as coaches and mentors. Further, they need to provide individual sales professionals with a reasonable amount of time to invest in personal mind-set development.

Stage 2: Validate and Refine the Model

Once the platform for Diagnostic Business Development is designed, it must be tested and refined. This is accomplished by using a pilot program.

We typically work with the head of sales to identify two or three sales teams (which may include a sales manager, one or more sales professionals, applications and technical support people, and sometimes a product manager). We identify three or four target opportunities for each team and then conduct a customized workshop to introduce the teams to the system, skills, and discipline of the new Diagnostic Business Development platform. In that workshop, each team plans how to approach its targeted prospective accounts.

By the end of the workshop, each team will have created a *diagnostic engagement planner*. This planner serves as a road map through the sales cycle and provides a mechanism for capturing critical information and feedback. When completed, the planner will be created for each prospective customer and include a tailored version of the *value hypothesis*, the *diagnostic agreement*, and the *diagnostic conversation strategy*.

Then a sales manager (sometimes accompanied by members of our firm) follows the teams through their sales engagements, evaluating the platform's viability and efficacy, and refining it based on the realities of working with actual customers. (During this stage, the sales teams engage with customers in a transparent way; in other words, they explain to the customer that they are conducting a pilot program with the intent of testing a model aimed at ensuring that the customer receives the greatest value potential from the relationship.)

Stage 3: Extend the Platform to the Entire Sales Force

Invariably, the pilot stage generates a number of success stories. These stories often include successful sales, but more importantly, the pilots open the team members' eyes to the potential of the new platform. They see how the new platform changes the flow of customer conversations and opens up access to people and information within customer organizations, and they bring those stories back to the sales organization at large. These stories serve as the basis for extending the platform to the entire sales organization—the third phase of the implementation process.

During stage 3, the Diagnostic Business Development platform is tailored as necessary for different solution sets and the different customer segments. This is usually accomplished very quickly once the initial platform is established and tested. Next, the rest of the sales organization needs the same development effort that the pilot teams received. Finally, employees in functions that are directly involved in the sales cycle should also learn the systems, skills, and disciplines. Typically this includes selected members of the marketing staff who are involved in creating sales collateral and generating leads, as well as support and service staff members who are involved in delivering and measuring customer value.

We should also pay particularly close attention to the critical role of line sales management while the capability is being established. First-line sales managers must model the new sales capability and hold salespeople accountable for adopting it, if it is to be successfully developed. Otherwise, most salespeople will dismiss the change, consider it the "flavor of the month," and assume that "this too shall pass," if they keep their collective heads down. To gain the support of line sales managers for the new capability, they must:

- **Learn it:** Line sales managers should be involved in the tailoring of the new capability and take personal ownership as early as possible in the planning stages. They should attend a sales development workshop before the capability is rolled out to the sales organization at large. They should also act as table coaches at the workshops that their sales teams attend.

- **Teach it:** The most effective way to engage line sales managers with the new capability is to ask them to conduct reinforcement training sessions for members of their sales teams. To provide a structure for this aspect of the implementation, we typically develop a series of 90-minute, manager-led sessions focused on one or two key aspects of the capability. These sessions are usually held once a month.

- **Coach it:** Coaching is a standard responsibility of sales managers, but most have never been taught how to coach effectively and have never been provided with a coaching process. To overcome these barriers, sales managers should attend workshops in which they learn the coaching skills specific to implementing a Diagnostic Business Development capability.

Hiring and Developing a World-Class Sales Organization

A capability is an odd duck in that it is embedded in an organization, but its success is largely dependent on people—that is, the group of people who exercise it. Individuals within the group will always utilize a capability with varying degrees of success, but ultimately, the more people who master and effectively use the capability, the more effective its results. For this reason, there is a large talent component to a Diagnostic Business Development capability, and the hiring, development, and retention of sales professionals are all critical issues in its success.

Hiring Diagnostic Sales Professionals

Perhaps more than any other business profession, success in sales is thought to be personality driven. Many people speak of the "born salesperson" as if the ability to sell is a genetic inheritance. Sales organizations implicitly subscribe to this view when they attempt to identify and hire people who exhibit the personality traits of the stereotypical salesperson. Many of them add industry experience to the job description and believe that is all that is needed to hire a winner. Often, they get a real winner . . . in a more sarcastic sense of the word.

Why do sales managers keep hiring salespeople based on stereotypical personality traits and industry experience? Because they don't have a systematic method of determining the true ingredients of Era 3 sales success, and thus have little choice but to fall back on what they've been conditioned to believe are the qualifications for exceptional performance. Sales managers in a Diagnostic Business Development environment, on the other hand, can hire based on the sales platform they are using and the capability that they are attempting to develop and support.

What kind of candidates should they be looking for? Individuals who can fulfill the role of a diagnostic sales professional—that is, people who can execute the system, learn and use the skills, and live the discipline.

Assessment instruments remain the best way to quickly and accurately obtain insight into the strengths and weaknesses of sales candidates. With that said, we need to be sure to carefully explore what the assessments we use actually measure. The vast majority of assessment instruments are one-dimensional, and they are aimed at identifying a conventional sales personality, which will point you toward the wrong candidates. In fact, if you run most top performers through a standard sales profiling tool, they will likely be rejected: they aren't aggressive enough, will take "no" for an answer, and won't push hard enough for the close.

To identify Prime sales candidates, we recommend combining three different kinds of assessments to create a holistic profile of the candidate and offer a high probability of predicting Diagnostic Business Development success:

1. A behavioral assessment that offers insight into a candidate's behavior style. This reflects "how" a candidate will sell. We are looking for candidates who portray the preferred behavior style that is a blend of the doctor, the best friend, and the detective.

2. An assessment that identifies the candidate's personal interests and values, which tells us "why" a candidate will sell. We are trying to understand the candidate's attitudes and motivations, and we are looking for the proverbial self-starter with a history of setting and achieving goals.

3. An assessment that provides insights into "what" the candidate can and will do relating to executing the Diagnostic Business Development process. This instrument provides an insight into the candidate's mental and emotional stamina. Does the candidate have the fortitude and strength needed to actually execute the system? We also gain insights into the professional growth potential of candidates and the type of development that may be most helpful to maximize their potential.

A 12-Stage Quick-Start Plan

Once we hire a candidate to work in a Diagnostic Business Development environment, we must teach the system, provide the skills, and coach the discipline that person needs to adopt and utilize the capability. Depending on the complexity of the sale, the solutions that our clients undertake, and the ability of the salesperson, the time requirements for training can vary widely, but they should follow a 12-stage sequence that we can define in terms of the questions each is designed to answer in the new hire's mind.

1. **What Is My Company All About?** Sales professionals need to know their company's history, the key people and positions, its market position, its value proposition, as well as the details of employment, such as the compensation plan, expense policies, and so forth.

2. **Who Are the Customers I Serve?** In this stage, new hires meet customers via the telephone and face-to-face appointments in the field. They learn the cast of characters, who buys from your company and, more importantly, why they buy, how they perceive your company, and how satisfied they have been with the value created by your company.

3. **How Do I Develop New Business?** After salespeople learn to prepare customer profiles, they need to understand how to prepare an opportunity management system that enables them to coordinate their activities and set priorities.

4. **What Is the Engagement Protocol?** In this stage, salespeople learn the basics of building an initial engagement strategy and a relevant value hypothesis from a prospect's profile.

5. **What Is My Personal Business Plan?** Individuals develop an initial version of an individualized business plan that includes their financial goals and specifies the quality and quantity of activities required to achieve those goals and the internal/external resources needed to help support those goals.

6. **What Are the Solutions I Sell?** During this stage, individuals learn much more than the technical features and benefits of your offerings. They learn how to

diagnose the indicators present in the absence of those features, and specific departments and job responsibilities in the customer's business in which to look for them. They also learn how to connect solutions to customers' business drivers.

7. **Can I Now Develop Business?** Salespeople begin applying their knowledge in the field. They prepare for and initiate new engagements, set qualified diagnostic appointments, and follow up on leads received. They remain closely supervised and are coached as necessary.

8. **Can I Diagnose the Customer's Situation?** In this stage, customer calls are conducted by the salesperson and an observer. They plan account strategy and prepare for and conduct diagnostic calls where they navigate the diagnostic conversation maps.

9. **Can I Determine the Cost of the Problem?** Salespeople extend the work of diagnosis with the customer in this stage. Problem consequences are established and the problem's financial impact is calculated.

10. **Am I Perceived as a Creative Problem Solver by My Customers?** In this stage, individuals learn and demonstrate the skills of solution design. They link and discuss solution options in terms of the problem, its total cost, the client's expectations for change, the risks involved, and the investment that customers are willing to make to achieve their expected outcomes.

11. **Can I Propose an Effective Solution?** In this stage, salespeople learn and demonstrate their ability to translate the customer's expectations into a compelling solution. They create a discussion document, gain confirmation, and translate that discussion document into a formal proposal.

12. **Can I Effectively Present a Proposal?** The final stage of a quick-start training program is demonstrating the knowledge required to review the proposal with the customer and complete the customer's decision process.

A quick-start training program should conclude with the salesperson's revision of his or her individual business plan. The revised plan should cover the next two quarters and include business and professional development goals; market, territory, and key customer analyses; targeted prospects; performance metrics; and resources needed to help achieve the goals. It should be a formal document agreed to by the salesperson and management. This business plan serves as the basis for performance monitoring, coaching, and review. These reviews should be conducted on a regular basis, weekly at first, and as the quality of the sales person's performance improves, biweekly, then monthly, and, eventually, once per quarter. Before each review, the salesperson should write a short (one- to two-page) summary of what's working, what's not working, and what needs to be changed, if anything, to stay on goal. By doing a self-analysis before meeting with the sales manager, development of self-management skills of the sales professional continues.

From Novice to Expert

Like any other professional, the development of a diagnostic sales professional never ends. It is a career-long quest that encompasses the continuous training, application, and refinement of a complete body of professional knowledge. The purpose of this ongoing training is the continuous improvement of a salesperson's ability to consistently operate the system, execute the skills, and adopt the disciplines of a professional. Its goal is improved closing rates, reduced proposal-to-close ratios, and optimization of the sales process.

When salespeople successfully complete quick-start training, they have established a firm foundation for their careers, but they are still what Stuart and Hubert Dreyfus, brothers and fellow professors at the University of California, would call "novices." With the support of the U.S. Air Force, the Dreyfus brothers studied the process of skill acquisition among aircraft pilots, race car drivers, and chess players. (Later, additional studies by other researchers extended their findings to the nursing profession.)[5] Their model of skill acquisition described five levels of professional development—from novice to expert—that can also be applied to sales. The progression describes a transition from a rigid adherence to taught rules and procedures through to an intuitive mode of behavior that relies heavily on deep, tacit understanding.

Novices are the new hires who may know little about business or sales. Novices must approach their new profession with an attitude of acceptance. They don't have the previous experience necessary to evaluate what they are learning; thus, they must accept the information they are offered and apply it without a complete understanding of the context in which they are working. They operate with a rigid adherence to rules, applying very little discretional judgment.

Advanced beginners have attained enough professional experience to begin to use their skills in a situational context. That is, they are starting to recognize aspects of situations, but they are still reacting within the guidelines of the skills themselves. They see all aspects of work treated separately and given equal importance. These individuals are not yet ready to operate without supervision.

Competent sales professionals understand most of the elements of the professional body of knowledge and can judge their responses in terms of specific situations. Professionals at this level can solve problems and efficiently organize and plan their own time. This is the point at which the 12-stage quick-start plan described previously leaves the new hire, but in contrast to what many learning theories suggest, this is not the endpoint in professional development.

Proficient sales professionals understand the customer's problem and its solution as a holistic process. They can discern what is most important in a situation. They are incorporating their experience into their performance and they can smoothly adapt their responses to changing situations.

Expert sales professionals represent the zenith of professional development. A good example of this is the top-performing sales professional who has a seemingly casual conversation with a customer and yet leaves the meeting with a complete picture of a newly identified problem or opportunity, a solution that is most likely to address it, and a strategy for moving the customer through the Prime Process. These sales professionals have a clear vision of what is possible and they have what it takes to turn that vision into reality.

The ultimate challenge in developing sales professionals is to move beyond competence and develop a sales organization of experts who have the capability to create value for their customers and capture an ample share of that value for their companies and themselves. A serious question that business leadership and sales management should be asking themselves is: "At what level of professional development described above does our current development program leave our sales team?"

Reality Check
Are You Creating General Practitioners or Specialists?

The complex sale requires salespeople who are experts in the problems that their customers face and their

(continued)

(*continued*)

solutions. Yet, we must acknowledge that there is a realistic limit to the capacity of even the most intelligent
individuals. We often find that salespeople in complex
environments are stretched too thin. They are responsible for either calling on too broad a range of customers or offering too broad a range of products and
services. In the former case, salespeople's ability to diagnose customers' problems is negatively impacted; in
the latter, their ability to design and deliver solutions
is negatively affected. Depth of knowledge is a key
characteristic of Diagnostic Business Development
professionals, and that requires a clear-headed view of
both the customer segments they serve and the range
of offerings they bring to market.

* * *

Creating a fully developed Diagnostic Business Development capability within the sales function will solve many of
the problems that companies face in Era 3, but sales is only
one small part of the corporate value chain. Sales can bring
value to customers—connecting it, quantifying it, and helping to achieve it—but if a company truly wants to optimize
the value it offers customers and capture the profitable
growth that will accrue in the process, its leaders need to
expand the Diagnostic Business Development capability
beyond the functional boundaries of sales. Why company
leaders should consider this challenge is the topic of the
next chapter.

Prevent Value Leakage

*Capture Your Value with Diagnostic
Business Development*

Value is the lifeblood of the business world. Value—in the form of improved efficiency, effectiveness, and ultimately, profit—is the only thing that business-to-business customers are interested in buying. Companies like yours seek to create differentiation and profitable growth by investing large amounts of money and time to create solutions that are capable of delivering value to these customers. But you cannot transform solutions into competitive advantage and profitable growth unless the customer actually improves business performance and can measure the achievement of the value that has been promised. You could say that you have achieved your goals when the sale is closed and can ignore customers' outcomes, but that is shortsighted: Customer success is the ultimate source of differentiation and profit. Your solution's value capability is not true value until your customer has achieved it.

With this in mind, I'd like to pose a question: *what percentage of the value capabilities of the solutions that your company creates and brings to market is actually transformed into profitable growth?* I've asked this question of senior executives in large and small companies in a wide variety of industries. Invariably, they aren't entirely sure how to answer the question. Most of them don't know what percentage of the value capabilities inherent in their solutions can be achieved by their customers and, as a result, be transformed into profitable growth. They understand and believe in their solutions, but they have assumed that because a value capability exists, enough customers will buy it and be able to achieve it, and therefore, it will reach their bottom line. The flaw in this assumption can be summed up in two words: *value leakage*.

Who Knows Where the Value Goes?

An easy way to grasp the concept of value leakage is to think of the value of a solution as a bucket full of water. When the solution is first conceptualized, the bucket is full. But, as it gets passed from function to function, on its way to the customer value sloshes out. As you will soon see, by the time it reaches the customer it is usually over three-quarters empty. That's value leakage.

Typically, the sales organization will take the brunt of the blame for value leakage, since the point of sale is where the results of the value leakage are most evident. However, the issue to examine is that the salesperson is actually left with very little value to sell. In fact, as you will see next, we are finding that over 80 percent of the value leakage has occurred by the time the solution is handed off to the salesperson.

Value leakage occurs throughout the value network as solutions move from conception to customer implementation.[1] Early in the process, value leakage happens as solutions are conceived, designed, and produced. Then, it occurs further as solutions are marketed and sold. Finally, it continues as companies seek to service and support their customers in their quest to achieve and measure the value capabilities promised by the solutions (see Figure 9.1).

Value leakage can begin from the very first glimmer of a new solution. This is because a solution's ultimate value is highly dependent on how well connected its creators are to the problems and opportunities that exist among their intended customers. Sometimes, a solution is very well connected to a customer problem—think of Wang's original word processor, FedEx's overnight delivery service, and Johnson & Johnson's cardiovascular stents. Sometimes, however, solutions are not well connected to their intended customers and the value exists mostly in the mind of the

Value Leakage

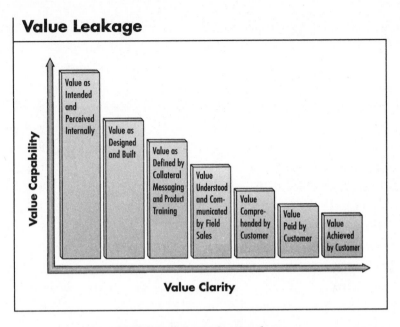

FIGURE 9.1 Value Leakage

inventor—think of Iridium, the original satellite phone system, and the Segway personal transporter, which businesses were supposed to buy in countless numbers.

Value leakage continues into the next stage in the value network—design engineering. In an ideal world, the designers add value capabilities to the solution by bringing the solution concept to life and refining it. In the real world, however, actual value often leaks away from the solution as the designers make trade-offs for the purposes of cost, quality, timing, and price without a clear understanding of the impact on the customer. Again, the less connected designers are with the solution's intended customers, the more value is at risk.

Now, the solution moves into production, where it runs headlong into the limitations of the manufacturing and purchasing processes. Value continues to leak as manufacturing demands design changes to force fit the solution into its existing facilities and assembly lines, again without understanding the consequences. More value leaks as procurement chooses low-cost suppliers for components and subassemblies, and grapples with delivery constraints.

Next, the solution moves into marketing, where the marketing communications and sales collateral required to attract customers is created. At this stage of the value chain, the leakage becomes more insidious because the investment to create the solution and its value capabilities has already been made and paid for. If the company's customers cannot see how to transform that potential value into reality, or if they can't determine why it is more valuable than a competitive offering, they will not buy your solution. Losses will begin to mount, and sometimes the company's very existence can be threatened. The value leakage in marketing all comes down to one root cause: the solution's value is not connected and quantified in a tangible and relevant way to the customer's world. Sometimes this happens because marketing places too much focus on meeting or exceeding competitors' claims; sometimes it happens because marketing is too focused on the features and benefits of the solution itself or generic value messages. In both cases, the mistaken assumption is that customers will be able to translate and differentiate the messages from competing messages in the marketplace and, as a result, will seek out and buy the solution. Instead, value leaks because competing solutions look and sound the same to customers who understand cost—commoditization ensues.

The value connections that marketing misses are invariably amplified in the sales organization. Value leaks because product-based sales training tends to be focused on long lists of features and benefits and/or generic messages. More leakage occurs as salespeople fail to comprehend the full value impact and present these generic messages to customers using conventional sales processes. Meanwhile, as in marketing, the efforts and resulting success to connect and quantify value to the customer's world in tangible and relevant terms is suboptimal. And, of course, customers are only willing to pay for the level of value that they are able to comprehend, which is usually far less than what the sales-person attempted to communicate and certainly less than the original designers envisioned.

If the sale is closed, the support and service functions work with customer companies to implement solutions and achieve their value. This becomes a struggle because customers often do not fully comprehend the value capability of the solutions they buy and/or the constraints that can keep them from achieving the value. So, more value leaks as implementations fail and unexpected costs are incurred, leading to frustrated customers and damaged relationships. As a result, the seller is unable to convert the sale to brand equity, referrals, and repeat business.

This may sound like an overly bleak assessment of how and where companies leak value, but it is not an exaggeration. When my firm tracks value leakage in client companies, we typically find that the companies are identifying less than one-half of the value that their solutions can actually deliver and they are able to quantify less than half of the value that they can identify. This suggests that the average business-to-business seller is going to market with 70 to 85 percent of the potential value of its solutions already lost. What makes this issue even worse, is that the 15 to 30 percent that they were able to clarify, is likely the same 15 to 30 percent that their competitors have clarified. This further exacerbates the commoditization challenge.

The results of these analyses tell us that the requirement to clarify value by connecting it to customers' performance metrics, and quantifying it, is not limited to the sales function. Business-to-business sellers need to sharpen their focus on value clarity and enhance customer value achievement in ways that are relevant and tangible by addressing value from their customers' perspectives (which might also include the value requirements of their customers) for all participants throughout the value network.

Key Thought
Uncertainty Defeats Decision
Making; Clarity Defeats Uncertainty.[1]

Customers are always uncertain regarding the issues that they should address and the actions they should take as they go about making complex decisions. If sellers do not provide a vehicle for achieving clarity and use it with their customers, it is highly unlikely customers will be able to achieve it on their own.

---

[1]Courtesy of Bob White, CEO, Lucidus, Ltd. (www.lucidus .co.uk).

Diagnostic Business Development
Prevents Value Leakage

I have already discussed how you can substantially enhance your company's sales results by developing Diagnostic Business Development into a functional capability that will enable your sales organization to help customers clarify and achieve value, but sales is only responsible for a short portion of the value chain. It cannot maximize value on its own. The sales organization does not create solutions. It does not procure the materials and services that go into the solutions. It does not manufacture solutions. It does not control the marketing of that value or the support services that ensure that customers will achieve the value they have purchased. All of these activities affect the flow of customer

value and the ability of your company to convert the value
it brings to market into profitable growth. Here's how Kris
Robinson, vice president of HP's recently established business intelligence unit, describes it:

> *It's not just about how you sell. It's the whole end-to-end
> alignment of the organization from a strategy perspective—
> from a marketing and value proposition perspective, from a
> portfolio perspective, from the perspective of sales execution,
> technical support, consulting and delivery, and whatever else
> you do. If you miss one of those pieces or a function has not
> bought in to the direction that you are trying to go, you can
> waste a lot of cycles trying to move the organization. You
> really have to get very, very strict up-front on understanding
> and defining your value capabilities and your differentiation.*

For these reasons, if you really want to optimize the
value that your company brings to market, you need to develop Diagnostic Business Development into an organizational capability. An organization-wide Diagnostic Business
Development capability prevents the erosion of value
because it positions the customer as the focal point of all
activity throughout the value network and *customer value* as
the primary driver of business performance. It is effective
because it ensures that everyone in the company understands
the value requirements of the company's intended customers
and how those requirements are connected to the value capabilities of the solutions it is bringing to market. The
development needs for a Diagnostic Business Development
capability vary with each function along your value network,
as described in subsequent sections.[2]

Research and Development

Traditionally, R&D has been guided by an egocentric principle, "If we build it, they will buy." It tended to be driven by

either technological capacity or the desire to out-innovate the competition. The result? Over 60 percent of potential new products never reach the market, and of those that do, about 40 percent fail to fulfill expectations.[3]

Today, R&D needs a new governing principle: "There is no such thing as a solution without a quantifiable problem that clarifies customer value." R&D must develop new products by first understanding the value drivers and performance metrics within the customer companies, and only then, move from the customer to the lab. This approach does not require that the customer be able to describe the new solution idea—or even the problem that the solution would address; I would never advocate self-diagnosis. What I am saying is any potential new solution must have a demonstrated value connection to a real customer. As Kris Robinson says:

> *It's very easy to define your solution portfolio in the context of what competitors in the market are doing. You look around and say, "Well, these guys are doing this and it sure would be easy to build a story around that because we can do it, too." The real magic is when you define where you think the customer can go and what's next, and you've got a defined process to help them get there. Then, you can get them to buy into the future state by solving the problem in manageable chunks.*

It's also not enough that a new idea for a solution impacts a single customer business driver in isolation from the customer's larger business. For example, a client company that designs and manufactures scientific instruments developed an innovative piece of test equipment that was able to test samples seven to nine times faster than any other instrument on the market. The only problem: it far outstripped the throughput capacity of the process used in customers' labs, so customers could not achieve the value capability of the instrument without making expensive changes to their internal processes. Not recognizing the constraints your customer must resolve to achieve the full value of your solution can be a huge source of value leakage. Recognizing those constraints and providing the ability to resolve them is a powerful source of differentiated value.

Marketing

Traditionally, the role of marketing has been to *communicate* the value that companies intend to deliver to market. The marketers would develop a value proposition, and then package it in advertising, promotional and PR campaigns, and sales collateral that described the features, benefits, and value of the solution. These materials tended to focus on the bright future that the customer would enjoy after purchasing the solution.

In Era 3, however, business-to-business sellers can no longer rely on customers to interpret that communication and make the connection between the value capabilities of the solutions and their value achievement. Sellers need to guide their customers to an understanding of this connection, and this guidance begins with marketing. Thus, marketing's primary role is to clarify value. This requires developing the system, skills, and discipline needed to connect each facet of a solution's value to the specific performance measurements in the customer's organization and develop the means for the sales force to quantify that value in a collaborative manner with the customer in such a way that the customer will "own" the resulting financial impact.

Marketing continues to develop sales aids and collateral, but with several key differences:

- Marketing materials must be much more targeted— to both market segments and to specific job responsibilities and performance metrics of executives within companies in each segment.

- Marketing materials must establish the foundation for a diagnosis-based, customer engagement flow that begins with a value hypothesis and asks the customer to consider the existence of evidence of the risks he or she may be facing (the negative present) *before* proceeding to his or her rosy future (the positive future). In other words, marketing should change its focus to the indicators of the business problems or opportunities that its solutions address.[4]

When the marketing department at Shell Global Solutions took a diagnostic approach to its work, it had a transformational effect, according to Wayne Hutchinson, then vice president of sales and marketing:

We put our marketers through the same diagnostic training as the sales force. They now use a diagnostic analytical process for everything they do.

The new way marketing organizes customer events is just outstanding. They go to the salespeople to find out what issues our customers are dealing with and want to hear about and then they get 50–100 high-powered executives from customer companies in a room for two or three days and engage them by discussing topics that are tailored perfectly to their challenges.

Marketing redesigned how it monitored, measured, and worked our branding in the press. We stopped placing articles and advertising focused on our technologies and products and instead began discussing the issues our customers are experiencing.

We also stopped trying to provide collateral for 850 different products and services and produced a few brochures that

*are focused on key early warning signs, problems and oppor-
tunities, and offering a value hypothesis.*[5]

Pre-Sale Technical Support

In the past, most business-to-business products and services were generally not complex enough to require formal
pre-sale technical support. That has changed as solutions
have become increasingly complex. In response, some companies have created sales teams in which the sales professional is responsible for the establishment and maintenance
of the customer relationship and a pre-sale support special-
ist manages the solution demonstration and presentation.

In Era 3, when technical support professionals play a key
role in sales engagements, they must also understand the
system, skills, and discipline of Diagnostic Business Development. Support professionals must recognize that their role
during the Diagnose phase is to assist in conducting a thorough diagnosis, and in the Design phase, they must assist in
the collaborative effort to design the optimal solution—as
opposed to simply presenting and explaining solutions.

Post-Sale Support

Traditionally, support has been a fundamentally reactive
function. When something failed, the customer called and
support fixed it (usually for a fee). Over time, this repair
service evolved into the service contract, which was sold
with the solution. Later, when the "hunter-farmer" model
of account management began to emerge, support was often assigned the role of the farmer, who tilled and harvested
existing accounts.

In Era 3, however, support needs to play a more pro-
active and integral part in value design and delivery. Support
professionals should be involved in the Design phase of the
Prime Process, and often should be given lead responsibility

after the deal is signed in the Deliver phase—ensuring that the customer achieves maximum value from the solution and is quantifying the value as it is achieved.

Because support professionals also tend to have regular and ongoing contact with the customer, they should also be responsible for monitoring the customer for the presence of new indicators that need to be addressed. One of our clients, a supplier of industrial gases, found many opportunities for new sales to existing customers when it put its delivery drivers through Diagnostic Business Development workshops. The drivers were taught how to spot indicators—physical symptoms of problems that this company could solve—as they made their deliveries to existing customers. Because they had broader and more regular access to customer operations, they were highly effective in spotting new business opportunities and passing that valuable information to the sales force.

* * *

Support functions, such as human resources and procurement, and a company's leadership team are also instrumental in creating value and converting it to profitable growth. Thus, they should also have the capacity to use Diagnostic Business Development.

Human Resources

Traditionally, human resources has been a compliance function. It hired and fired employees, made sure that their paperwork was properly processed, paid and taxed them, and promoted and sometimes fired them in accordance with the myriad laws and regulations.

Today, HR has a much more critical role as the organization's chief talent developer and manager, and a center of excellence for capability building. In these roles, HR is responsible for fostering a Diagnostic Business Development culture within the organization.

It also plays a key support role in ensuring that every function has the right talent in the right place at the right time. Human resources needs to understand the system, skills, and discipline of Diagnostic Business Development in order to establish a hiring profile and clearly describe the job requirements to candidates. This is especially important in sales, where HR can help shape the sales force itself—facilitating the outplacement of salespeople who cannot or will not adopt the Diagnostic Business Development approach (which can be 20 to 30 percent of the sales force, in my experience), and helping sales leaders recruit, develop, and retain sales professionals who can flourish in the new environment.

Procurement

Traditionally, the role of procurement has been analogous to the immune system in the human body: It was charged with protecting the organization from opportunistic outsiders (typically, salespeople) and obtaining the materials and components needed to create solutions at a cost that maximized the company's margins. Procurement accomplished this by adopting a standardized one-size-fits-all buying process that forces all those who wanted to do business with the company into an apples-to-apples comparison, whether they were selling paper clips or scarce resources of strategic importance.

Today in Era 3, this focus on insulating the organization from the outside and driving down suppliers' prices has been proven shortsighted. It strips value from solutions by cutting off access to high-value innovative suppliers and raises total costs. Instead, the role of procurement should be to optimize value throughout the value chain.

Procurement can prevent value leakage between the supplier and the firm by monitoring and managing the value delivered by suppliers. In fact, it can actually help create incremental value by teaching the Diagnostic Business Development approach to the company's operational managers and its suppliers, so the organization can buy in the same way that it sells to its customers. Wayne Hutchinson has been implementing such an approach at Shell International. He explains it like this:

> *You create value in procurement by working with suppliers just as you would create value for a customer in the sales process. We've done this with a major supplier of gas turbines that cost tens of millions of dollars. We worked with them to analyze everything from bidding and winning contracts, to the design, manufacture, and installation of the turbines. As a result, we cut the delivery time on these critical path components in half, and this has created multiples of the value that simple cost reductions would provide, for both us and our supplier. Now that we've won the suppliers' trust and taught them how to sell to us, we are engaging in exactly the same way to work on reducing other costs in how we work together, again, creating value for both of us.*

A Source of Organizational Alignment and Learning

An organization-wide Diagnostic Business Development capability prevents value leakage and serves as a powerful enabler of value and profitable growth for two reasons. First, it is a linking mechanism that is capable of generating value alignment, deployment, and measurement within the organization. Everyone in the organization will be speaking the same language and working in a coordinated fashion toward the realization of customer value. Second, it is a mechanism for communicating and applying the learning that is generated as the value the company produces bumps up against the realities of the marketplace.

Strategic Alignment

The modern corporation depends on the division of labor. Around the time of the American Revolution, Adam Smith glowingly described the efficiencies inherent in labor specialization using the example of a pin factory, in which he showed how 10 workers could raise their output from fewer than 200 pins per day to more than 48,000 pins by simply assigning one worker to each task in the production process.[6] Specialization enabled the growth of huge companies, but it also had a downside that Smith did not anticipate. Specialists don't always see the big picture and they often have conflicting goals.

The division of labor created boundaries between functions, and when those boundaries become barriers to overall performance, they create what has come to be called the *silo effect*. When companies suffer from the silo effect, value creation is negatively affected. Value formulation and delivery are segmented and isolated into functions. One department completes its work in isolation from the other functions within the company and tosses it over the wall into the next function. Each successive department does the same until the goal is achieved.

In today's complex organizations, this isolation is one of the primary causes behind the failure of corporate value initiatives. The most common results of the cross-functional dysfunction created by the silo effect are inefficient execution, inhibited communication, shallow thinking, and slowed response times to customers and the marketplace. For instance, I've seen engineers create new products with little or no input from the rest of the organization and even without the input of customers;

marketers create advertising campaigns and value messaging in a vacuum; and salespeople uncover major customer needs and fail to report them.

What's missing here is the alignment of functions around corporate value creation. Whether you are buying or selling (whatever role you are playing in the value exchange), Diagnostic Business Development is a mechanism for creating a cohesive, cross-functional team that communicates and reinforces strategy, gets everyone working toward the same goal, and measures net value achieved. Everyone in the organization should be concerned with how to create value and leverage it for corporate and customer success. Everyone should feel a responsibility for the welfare of the organization as a whole and its customers. Here's how Greg Lewin, former president of Shell Global Solutions, describes the focusing effect of customer value and Diagnostic Business Development:

> *The model that we used in Global Solutions was a globe that had the customer at the center of our world. Delivering value to the customer became a shared vision. All of the vice presidents knew that if there was tension between them, I would start by telling them that this is all about delivering value to the customer and how we can best accomplish that. No matter what the issue was, they knew that the customer was where I was going to start. When we did our strategy-away days and our operational meetings, the customer is where we started. When we worked on technology or efficiency or delivery issues, the customer is where we started.*

Organizational change is difficult in the best of times. You need to use every means that you can to achieve it. The most powerful forces are market forces and customers, and if you expose the organization to them, it will drive change. By starting with the customer—and I think you can start with the customer in any business problem—a lot of the internal turf stuff either becomes so blatant or so dysfunctional that it drops away immediately.

The four phases of the Diagnostic Business Development system—Discover, Diagnose, Design, and Deliver—offer a single, customer-centered process through which each function can explore the value opportunities in the marketplace and ensure that its efforts are aligned with the rest of the company and its intended customers.

The pharmaceutical industry is a good model of how this alignment can play out in the real world. When the R&D function of a prescription drug maker undertakes the creation of a new product, it uses a process that can be framed around the four phases of the Prime Process. R&D seeks to *discover* a market of patients that is large enough to support the investment required to create a new drug. It *diagnoses* the physical symptoms, causes, and consequences of patients' problems. It seeks to *design* a drug that will best solve the problems, including recognizing the side effects (constraints to value) that the patient may experience. And it *delivers* the new drug through a highly regulated process of testing and government approvals.

The process is repeated as the drug maker's marketers and then its sales professionals create and align their efforts to bring the drug to the health-care providers who will prescribe it. This time, the discovery process is used to segment and refine the markets for the drug. The indicators of each segment are diagnosed, the solution design is altered to fit each, and the solution is delivered.

The doctors who prescribe the medication repeat the Prime Process yet again. They discover at-risk patients by matching them to the profile of patients who are likely to need the drug, diagnose the individual patient, design the proper dosage and related therapy, and then prescribe the best solution and monitor the patient's compliance to the therapy and his or her progress throughout the delivery phase.

Each cycle of the Prime Process builds on the one before it; each is aligned with and supports the total effort. These same four phases can be applied to the value proposition of any product or service that grows out of a corporate strategy. In the absence of the Prime Process, there is significant value leakage as the organization moves from creating a strategy to achieving results.

Organizational Learning

The second mechanism that derives from the Diagnostic Business Development capability is an organizational capacity for learning. MIT's Peter Senge popularized the idea of the learning organization in the early 1990s. A learning organization, he wrote, is an organization where people continually expand their capacity to create the results they truly desire, where new and expansive patterns of thinking are nurtured, where collective aspiration is set free, and where people are continually learning how to learn together.[7]

Interestingly, when Senge identified the seven learning disabilities common in today's organizations, the first was the fact that employees tend to identify with their jobs and limit their loyalty to their functional responsibilities. This identification and loyalty, said Senge, does not extend to the purpose and vision of the larger organization. The silo effect and cross-functional dysfunction strike again!

The problem, of course, is that when learning is stifled, so is the ability of the organization to adequately adapt its value capabilities and respond to its customers' value requirements. This ultimately negatively impacts a company's ability to retain customers and create profitable growth.

Whether an organization must respond to new value opportunities, make changes in the market environment, or correct miscalculations in its current value strategy, it must have a mechanism capable of capturing and responding to feedback. It needs to be able to identify, communicate, and respond to the customer's situation throughout the value creation process. Diagnostic Business Development serves as that mechanism.

The Prime Process requires that the various functions within the organization that are responsible for delivering value to customers take to the field in one voice and one process. To effectively Discover, Diagnose, Design, and Deliver value, they frame their assumptions in terms of the customer, and they test those assumptions against the reality of the customer's world. We want the scientists in R&D to view their ideas and creations through their customer's eyes via the Prime Process. We want to push marketing and product development out into the real world where they can directly observe the symptoms of the absence of value, and experience firsthand the challenges their customers are facing. We want sales professionals to communicate the issues they uncover as they conduct a diagnosis, and we want service and support staff to report the issues they find during the delivery and implementation of solutions. This ongoing diagnostic feedback loop creates a learning flow that, in turn, can be used to generate continuous value improvement and breakthrough value innovation.

How might this play out in the everyday world of business? Picture a financial software developer that has a 250-member sales force calling on CFOs around the world. As the salespeople are busy diagnosing the problems that their prospects are experiencing, they are collecting valuable information. If at the end of a month, they report back that 76 percent of the CFOs they have called on are experiencing and have identified "issue X" as their greatest concern, and relay that information to marketing, how soon can 50,000 messages aimed at CFOs having trouble with "issue X" be delivered? If the company's software does not already address "issue X," how soon after the information is delivered can an existing product be modified or a new one be developed that can deliver the value? The crucial point: none of this can happen without a learning mechanism.

The Value-Driven Company

Diagnostic Business Development offers a framework for the creation of value (see Figure 9.2). An organization's concept of value grows out of its vision. This vision provides the

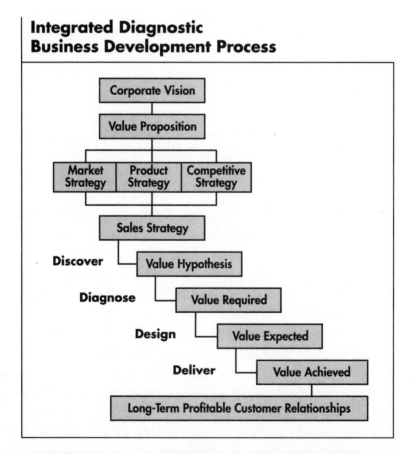

FIGURE 9.2 Integrated Diagnostic Business Development Process

foundation from which a value proposition is derived and corporate strategy evolves. The value proposition, along with the products and services it generates, is delivered to the customer through a series of strategies that together comprise a go-to-market strategy. The foundational belief of this framework is that the value achieved by the customer is the primary measurement of business performance.

The market strategy defines the marketplace in which the company will do business. It identifies the markets and market segments in which the company will sell its products and services. The competitive strategy defines a company's position with regard to other organizations within its market spaces. It identifies other companies vying for business in the same marketplaces, evaluates their strengths and weaknesses, and offers a plan to successfully compete against them. The product strategy defines the company's products and services. It determines how each will fit the particular market segment for which it is designed. Finally, sales strategy defines how the company's product and services will be offered to customers. The sales strategy is created at three levels: the customer or enterprise level, the opportunity level, and the individual or appointment level. It details the content and flow of the sales process and diagnostic strategy, and it is defined by the market, competition, and product strategy. This is why an organizational capacity for Diagnostic Business Development is critical to successful sales execution.

The corporate value proposition is the foundation for each of the four strategies: market, competitive, product, and sales. The purpose of these strategies is to deliver the promise of the value proposition to market and, ultimately, value achievement to individual customers. Through them, the value proposition is extended to the market, yielding a hypothesis about customers' situations and the ability of the company's offerings to address those issues; the value hypothesis is explored, yielding clarity about the problems being experienced and the value required by the customer. This leads to the collaborative design of the best solutions and the value expected from implementing those solutions; and the value capability is delivered and, in turn, yields value achievement for both the buyer and the seller. Value has successfully been exchanged and measured.

The Diagnostic Business Development process is traveled twice in the creation and delivery of value. The first pass through the process occurs as each of the four strategies under the Value Life Cycle is developed. In this way, a company can ensure that each element of its strategic plan for creating value is aligned with prospective customers' business requirements and leveraged at the product, process, and performance levels of customer companies. In other words, we want to be sure that our strategies are capable of delivering value before we devote costly resources to pursuing them.

The second pass through the Diagnostic Business Development process occurs during the execution of each of the four strategies. In this pass, a company ensures that each strategy actually works as planned and makes any necessary corrections in real time. In other words, we want to ensure that each strategy is capable of fulfilling the value proposition we are bringing to market and creates the expected value hypothesis, value requirements, value expectations, and value achievement.

When the Diagnostic Business Development process is successfully traversed, value is realized, delivered to customers, and returned to the company in the form of increased profits. The by-product of this end result is the lifeblood of corporate success—value, in the form of long-term, profitable customer relationships. The corporate vision has been transformed into bottom-line results.

Epilogue
The Era 3 Sales Future

*You Can Watch It Happen to You or You Can Make
It Happen for You*

The same two forces that are driving today's Era 3 sales environment are also shaping the structure and focus of tomorrow's sales world: commoditization and complexity. They have split the world of sales into two distinct arenas and a chasm continues to widen. On one side of the split, selling has become a self-service, commodity-based, cost-driven transaction—a non-prescription sale. On the other side, the typical sale is a complex, value-driven trans-action—a prescription sale that continues to require the guidance of an experienced team of business advisors.

Conventional selling strategies and tactics are no longer effective on either side. There is no reason to sell at all on the commodity side of the chasm. Customers have access to all the product information they need. They can diagnose their problems, design their solutions, and serve themselves. As a result, comparisons on price, convenience, and transaction cost become the driving force in the market. There isn't any room for a dedicated sales force in the non-prescription, commodity sale. In fact, a sales organization is an unnecessary and high-risk expense. When salespeople are not adding value via the diagnosis, design, and delivery of value, their presence can't be justified.

On the other side of the chasm is the complex sale. This sale cannot be managed as a self-service transaction. The customer situations and the competing solutions that address them are difficult to understand, analyze, and evaluate. In fact, because of advances in technology and rising competitive pressures, complex sales are becoming even more complex—they are increasingly difficult to manage. The more complex problems and solutions become on this side of the chasm, the less likely it is that they can be sold using conventional sales practices or a self-serve transaction. Customers simply do not have the knowledge or resources necessary to self-diagnose their situations or de-sign and implement solutions. They require the assistance and support of highly skilled sales professionals.

Choose a Side

The interesting thing about the splitting of the sales world is that companies have a large degree of choice about whether to bring their offerings to market using either the commodity model or the complex model. They can decide which side their services and products will occupy.

Some companies, especially in the business-to-business sector, do not fall cleanly into a commodity or complex transaction. They are already straddling the chasm and can either choose one selling model for their entire organiza-tion or clearly segment their markets and products into one of the two models. Other companies are operating in markets that are already defined as either commodity markets or complex markets. But that doesn't mean that they can't change their business model and switch sides.

The question you need to answer is: "Which model should my company pursue?"

There is no simple answer to this question. If your company can squeeze more cost out of the system than your competitors can, competing in the commodity sale may be a viable choice. Certainly, there are companies that have become very successful by sticking to a low-cost, high-volume strategy. Competing on price is, however, a two-edged sword. As soon as someone else figures out a way to beat your price, customers will switch their allegiance.

I believe that a value-creation sales model ultimately offers a far more profitable opportunity than a price-based sales model. It is the complex sale that offers the opportunity to create the most value for your customer and capture the most value for your organization. The complex sale allows you to differentiate your company and capture and defend a competitive advantage in the marketplace. For all of these reasons, organizations that have a choice would do well to embrace and develop a complex sales model.

The two key issues for those who choose the complex sale then become:

1. Can you create, connect, and quantify value for your customers and capture a share of that value for your organization and yourself?

2. Do you have a process that allows your customers to comprehend the absence of that value in their businesses and create the willingness to pay a reasonable premium in price to receive that value?

Shape Your Future

For those who choose to pursue a high-value strategy, the final advice I would offer is to move quickly to embrace the Diagnostic Business Development selling model described in this book and secure your future. As with most strategies, the companies that take the lead in shaping the sales environment in which they operate are more likely to succeed than those who follow the leaders.

The hard reality of the marketplace dictates that you are either part of your system or somebody else's. If you are working your system, you are in control of your destiny. If you are in the latter, odds are you will end up a victim.

The Diagnostic Business Development process enables you to clearly differentiate yourself from the competition early, and it creates value through the selling process itself. The ability to make a high-quality decision is not a common capability among customers in the complex environment. It is the value the Prime Process creates and captures that gives it the power to define our customers' expectations and shape our marketplaces.

Sales professionals who are equipped with the systems, skills, and disciplines of the Diagnostic Business Development platform can bring a value-based decision process to even the most complex customer's situation and will establish a position in their customers' minds that competitors, especially those with conventional salespeople, will find hard to dislodge. Consider your past experience with salespeople. What outcomes characterized your most positive buying experiences? For me, the best buying experiences have been those in which a sales professional asked me questions I had not thought of. He or she expanded my thinking and helped me reach a high-quality decision with all that it implies—no matter what the product or service I was purchasing.

Ultimately, there are three selling systems vying for supremacy in any particular sales engagement: the customer's system, the competitor's system, and your system. You can get caught up in the customer's system; in fact, that is the primary pitfall of conventional selling systems. The problem is that customer systems are flawed, and as such, deteriorate to criteria dominated by the lowest common denominator—price—and rarely lead to a high-quality decision. You can fall prey to your competitor's selling system, but, of course, it is designed to the competitor's advantage. As a result, you will find yourself constantly defending your value against its smoke and mirrors and even when you win, you will face price pressures. Finally, you can bring your own system to the complex sale.

This last alternative is always the best. When you provide the decision system, you have the highest degree of professional control over the results. When that system is the Diagnostic Business Development platform, you are well on your way to *mastering the complex sale* and being able to *compete and win when the stakes are high*.

Allow me to leave you with one final key thought: Whenever you watch a pro doing what they do best—whether it is one of the world's best athletes, an accomplished musician, an extraordinary physician, a successful entrepreneur, or a high-performing sales professional—it often looks like that person is performing magic. He or she is not. His or her performance is based on systems, skills, and, above all, discipline. The spectacular successes that you see are always preceded by unspectacular but committed and comprehensive preparation that you don't see. When you take a look behind the curtain, you will see—there is no magic.

Key Thought
There Is No Magic!

Spectacular success is always preceded by unspectacular preparation.

So enjoy your preparation and enjoy your success!

About Prime Resource Group

Books by Jeff Thull

Strategy

The Prime Solution: Close the Value Gap, Increase Margins, and Win the Complex Sale

- The executive's guide to world-class performance and profitability
- An integrated, cross-functional approach to "close the value gap"
- Turn value fulfillment into a core competency

Process

Mastering the Complex Sale: How to Compete and Win When the Stakes Are High

- Systems, skills, and disciplines for winning high-stakes sales in a complex and evolving market
- Connect at the levels of power, influence, and decision
- Stop commoditization and get paid for your valuable solutions

Execution

Exceptional Selling: How the Best Connect and Win in High Stakes Sales

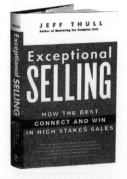

- From "first calls" to the "C-suite" plus everything in between—a step-by-step guide to the most important conversations you can have
- Build credibility and trust—become a valuable resource for your customers
- Powerful one-on-one diagnostic conversations magnificently orchestrated in a straight-talk book

Translating Market Strategy into Sales Results

About Prime Resource Group

From strategic solutions to tactical sales training, from field implementation to the deployment of complex solutions and product launches, Prime Resource Group's customized business transformation and performance improvement programs optimize and execute go-to-market strategies.

Jeff Thull, CEO and President of Prime Resource Group, and Prime's team of Senior Consultants and Managing Directors, work with global corporations across functions and business cultures to help connect and quantify their complex solutions to their customers' business drivers.

Prime Resource Group's ultimate purpose in each engagement is to create and implement systems, skills, and disciplines that will improve commitment, performance, and profitability. The highly customized programs, products, and services ensure that clients acquire, expand, and retain long-term and profitable customer relationships built on credibility, trust, and mutual respect.

For more information about Prime Resource Group's services, visit our web site at www.primeresource.com, contact Customer Support at 1-763-473-7529, or e-mail support@primeresource.com.

Diagnostic Business Development® Programs Customized and Connected to Your Customer's World

Keynote Address by Jeff Thull, CEO and President of Prime Resource Group

Powerful, entertaining, and highly customized to your audience.

Diagnostic Selling®

Diagnostic Selling develops the mind-set and diagnostic communication skills required to manage quality decisions and build strong relationships based on trust and credibility at all levels of decision and influence within the customer's organization.

Mastering the Complex Sale®

Mastering the Complex Sale delivers the skills required to build organization-to-organization relationships. Participants identify key business issues at the functional and corporate level, quantify business problems, identify the cost and risk of change, and establish sustainable partnerships with customers.

Mastering Executive Relationships®

Mastering Executive Relationships focuses on the shift of power and influence to the executive level. You will gain access and establish credibility by connecting quantified value to the executive's strategic objectives.

Prime Performance Leadership®

The Prime Performance Leadership program gives managers the tools and process to select, develop, and lead a world-class sales organization. Managers will sharpen critical management issues and make impressive gains in performance and bottom-line results.

Manager-Led Sales Performance Leadership

This program puts managers in control. Prime Resource Group delivers its expertise to your management team, as well as providing the instruction and tools for managers to take that expertise to lead and develop their teams with a continuous improvement process. The format integrates leadership and coaching skills with sales strategy and process to create world-class organizations that can win more profitable and repeatable sales.

Diagnostic Marketing®

Prime Resource Group's Diagnostic Marketing program helps companies build an integrated cross-function business development program that builds and coordinates sales collateral and messaging that clearly supports sales and connects to your customer's business drivers. It creates strategic alignment between marketing, product development, sales, and support.

Strategic Value Performance Assessment

The Strategic Value Performance Assessment process clarifies, validates, and quantifies value, and connects it at all levels of decision and influence in the customer's organization. It enables the alignment of resources to connect complex solutions to your customers' performance metrics and quantify the amount of value delivered to your customer.

Strategic Account Planning

This program organizes teams around national and global strategic accounts. It gives sales and marketing professionals the best opportunity to capitalize on the most lucrative opportunities. It provides a systematic approach that becomes a framework for planning and prioritizing actions that lead to clear decisions for winning high-stakes sales.

Key Moments of Value®

Critical interactions with customers take place at all function levels within an organization. At any moment in day-to-day activity, any individual can make a major impact on customers that can either build customer confidence, respect, and loyalty, or undermine the best efforts of the organization as a whole. Key Moments of Value helps entire organizations raise the bar of excellence.

Notes

Chapter 1

1. John Sullivan first described the three eras in a survey of sales training material that he researched for a course he taught at the University of Minnesota. You can download a copy of the foreword or view a video clip of a keynote for a quick overview of the three eras at our web site, www.primeresource.com.

2. Clayton M. Christensen, *The Innovator's Dilemma* (Boston: Harvard Business School Press, 1997), p. xxiii.

3. See Sam I. Hill, Jack McGrath, and Sandeep Dayal, "How to Brand Sand," *strategy + business*, April 1, 1998.

4. Brendan Matthews, "Plane Crazy: The Joint Strike Fighter Story," *Bulletin of the Atomic Scientists* (May/June 1998).

5. Christopher Helman, "ExxonMobil: Green Company of the Year," *Forbes.com*, August 24, 2009.

Chapter 2

1. Geoffrey A. Moore, *Crossing the Chasm: Marketing and Selling High-Tech Products to Mainstream Customers* (New York: Harper Business, 1999).

2. Bill Lucas, *Power Up Your Mind: Learn Faster, Work Smarter* (London and Naperville, IL: Nicholas Brealey, 2001), p. 126.

Chapter 3

1. William T. Brooks and Thomas M. Travisano, *You're Working Too Hard to Make the Sale* (Homewood, IL: Irwin, 1995), p. 16.

2. In *The Trusted Advisor* (New York: Free Press, 2000), David Maister, Charlie Green, and Robert Galford devoted a full chapter to the effectiveness of the Columbo model for consultants. They also rightly note that the main barrier to using this model is the emotional need to be the center of attention.

Chapter 4

1. If you would like to see how to analyze a CEO's letter to shareholders in order to craft an effective value hypothesis and letter of introduction, I've posted an example using the CEO's message published in a recent General Mills annual report on our web site at www.mcsbook.com.

2. Three years after the first edition of this book was released, I wrote a book titled *Exceptional Selling: How the Best Connect and Win in High Stakes Sales* (Wiley, 2006). It is devoted to the conversational tools and techniques that support the complex sale in each of its four stages. You can read the first chapter on our web site at www.primeresource.com.

Chapter 5

1. Dr. Sacks' quote appeared in *Forbes*, August 21, 2000.

2. Avery Comarow, "America's Best Hospitals: The 2009–10 Honor Roll," *U.S. News & World Report*, July 15, 2009, http://health.usnews.com/articles/health/best-hospitals/2009/07/15/americas-best-hospitals-the-2009-2010-honor-roll.html.

Chapter 6

1. I often use the term "trusted advisor" as a synonym for "valued business advisor," so I'd like to acknowledge *The Trusted Advisor* (New York: Free Press, 2000) by David H. Maister, Charles H. Green, and Robert M. Galford.

Chapter 7

1. Fred Reichheld, *The Ultimate Question: Driving Good Profits and True Growth* (Boston: Harvard Business Press, 2006), p. 15.
2. Donna Greiner and Theodore Kinni, *1,001 Ways to Keep Customers Coming Back* (New York: Three Rivers Press, 1999), p. 128.

Chapter 8

1. Joe Gibbs with Ken Abraham, *Racing to Win: Establish Your Game Plan for Success* (Sister, OR: Multnomah Books, 2002), p. 267.
2. Peter F. Drucker, *Management: Tasks, Responsibilities, Practices* (New York: Harper and Row, 1973), p. 64.
3. Shumeet Banerji, Paul Leinwand, and Cesare Mainardi, *Cut Costs, Grow Stronger* (Cambridge, MA: Harvard Business Press, 2009), p. 12.
4. Sullenberger's February 9, 2009, interview on CBS News's *60 Minutes* can be seen online at www.cbsnews.com/video/watch/?id=4784012n.
5. Patricia Benner, *From Novice to Expert* (Reading, MA: Addison-Wesley, 1984).

Chapter 9

1. Many of the activities in the value network occur concurrently and interdependently, but for clarity, I am portraying them in a linear fashion.

2. Because the application of Diagnostic Business Development in the sales function has been discussed at length in the rest of the book, I won't repeat it here.

3. Clayton M. Christensen and Michael Raynor, *The Innovator's Dilemma* (Boston: Harvard Business School Press, 2003), p. 73.

4. If you would like guidelines for this value translation, visit www .mcsbook.com or see the Value Translation Questionnaire, *The Prime Solution* (New York: Kaplan Business, 2005), p. 158.

5. For specific examples, view Shell Global Solutions' web site at www.shell.com/home/content/global_solutions/.

6. Adam Smith, *An Inquiry into the Nature and Causes of the Wealth of Nations* (www.gutenberg.org/etext/3300).

7. Peter M. Senge, *The Fifth Discipline: The Art and Practice of the Learning Organization* (New York: Doubleday, 1990).

Index